Just a Minute, Mrs. Gulliver

Being the account of the travels and travails of one Mrs. Bob Considine in the wicked cities of the world, wherein the wacky doings of high and low are hilariously set forth

by
Millie Considine

Prentice-Hall, Inc., Englewood Cliffs, N. J.

None of the characters in this book is fictitious
and any resemblance to any persons dead or alive
is purely inevitable. I just hope none of the friends
I mention herein minds being included in my life.
Please lay any shadings of absolute truth to the
fallibility of human memory, especially mine.
You'll notice the simple language and the absence
of such words as aberglaube, exiguous, prestidigi-
tator, dochandorris, ratiocinate, stramineous, etc.,
all of which would have fit into the text beautifully here and there . . . but I *do* want my
kids and Toots Shor to be able to read the book!

Library of Congress Catalog Card Number: 67–15167
Printed in the United States of America
T 51400

Prentice-Hall International, Inc., *London*
Prentice-Hall of Australia, Pty. Ltd., *Sydney*
Prentice-Hall of Canada, Ltd., *Toronto*
Prentice-Hall of India Private Ltd., *New Delhi*
Prentice-Hall of Japan, Inc., *Tokyo*

For Bob

I am indebted to DIPLOMAT Magazine and the MORNING TELEGRAPH (Triangle Publications, Inc.) for allowing me to draw on some of the columns I wrote for them . . . also to my great friend Louis Lurie of San Francisco for suggesting the title of the book.

Contents

Introduction

✿§❧✿ Living with Millie can be a bit difficult, at times. Nothing serious, really. Little things like a dinner last Fall at the Plaza for the benefit of Fu Jen University on Taiwan. Being essentially a generous dame, Millie gets herself involved in such exotic charities. Her friends follow her blindly through these follies, often at $50 a plate. But for recompense they want more than the broiled chicken and the boiled speeches. They want Millie. This was brought home abruptly to me at the Fu Jen-fest. I saw one of our friends at the cocktail party that preceded the dinner and fixed upon her the benign gaze and cheerful salute that has made me the toast of the Continent.*

"Where's Millie?" the dear old battle-axe demanded.

I said with great pride that my wife had turned her back on this great humanitarian bacchanal to appear at our daughter's school's Parents Day.

"Then to Hell with Fu Jen University," she said. "If Millie isn't here, I'm leaving."

Which she did. But I don't think she should have stepped on my toe as she swept past me. After all, I'm related to Millie. By marriage.

But that's the story of my life. People prefer Millie, and I've long since come to the conclusion that such people can't be all bad. They simply prefer a pretty gal who can tell a story, keep it short, and deliver the punch-line with sparkling emphasis and

* Antarctica.

clarity. There aren't very many girls like that. Matter of fact, they are as rare as female chefs. Besides, she dresses better than I do.

In the newspaper business I'm fairly well-known as a stiff who travels more to far-off lands in search of stories than almost anyone else. On many occasions I've been able to arrange for Millie to come along with me, frequently at considerable cost. Now, a husband instinctively wants to be looked on as the saltiest salt of the earth if he has sufficient love and dough to take his wife with him on a business trip. But there's precious little opportunity to take any bows when the word spreads that Millie is on the move again.

"Sure envy your wife, making that great trip to Australia to cover the Olympic Games," people said. "Too bad you can't make it, being a sportswriter."

"But I *am* making it," I'd say. "I'm covering it."

"You mean you're going with Millie?"

"No, dammit, she's going with *me*. I'm the one who is assigned." I'd find my voice rising. And more often than not, our mutual friends would leave this shrill scene a bit upset by my manner.

"I don't know why he's so touchy about Millie taking him to Australia with her," one said.

I used to write about Millie now and then, but not so much any more. There's a point at which you knock off. The object of your affection just doesn't want to be exposed in print as someone who split a martini with Herbert Hoover. It is always a touch-and-go proposition when you write about your family. If you're too saccharine, all the readers throw up. If you're casually cynical, the Stillness of Appomattox sets in around the house. Had a trying experience with our daughter Debbie once after writing about how her Christmas list so perfectly betokened the dear and sensitive age period through which she was passing, half Awakened, half Tomboy. She had listed these wishes: A New Party Dress, A New Hat, A Ring with a Green Stone, A Junior Miss Brassiere, and A Football. Debbie was indignant when my column appeared. I could never understand why she got so upset over my writing that she wanted A New Party Dress.

I guess the best piece I did about Millie went this way:

A girl I know named Millie will be married 25 years tomorrow. You don't meet many people like that in the set in which she travels. Some of her friends who have been married only a few times less than Man O' War regard her not only with affection but the awe reserved generally for the Pioneer Woman.

Millie has had only one husband, has two blue eyes, can write with one hand tied behind her back, has four children, and carries five pieces of luggage on trips as short as the ladies room at "21." She considers six her lucky number.

In a climate wherein some of her friends change jewels between courses at dinner, like the wines, her jewels consist entirely of several barely visible diamond chips in her wedding ring. She couldn't care less.

There was a time, though, when she did own a big star sapphire. A friend brought it to her from Ceylon during the war. But one of the children was playing with it in the bathroom one day and wondered if it would flush. It did.

Millie can work all day on her columns and articles, pay the bills, stall them pleasantly when there isn't enough to go around, cook, answer 419 phone calls, shop for the kids, have dinner with them, help with their homework (she was a magna come loudly in college), hear their prayers, get to a theater just as the curtain rises, dance like a swan at El Morocco until all hours,

get a few hours sleep, and be as good as new the next day. She
has easily scored hundreds of decisions over that most menacing
bruiser known to modern society, the cocktail party.

Not many women tell jokes well. But Millie does. Not many
girls shake hands honestly—as a good man shakes hands. Millie
does. Not many people can laugh gracefully at the top of their
lungs. Millie can, and will.

She is probably the most traveled person ever born in Coyle,
Okla. She knows the headwaiter at Maxim's in Paris as well as
she knows the short order cook at Schultz's drugstore in Allenhurst, N. J.

The schools she attended in Kansas City, Kans., and Mo., are
not renowned for their language courses, yet their sweet girl
graduate almost instantly picks up enough of the language of
each country she visits to supply herself with the basic needs of
life and keep her traveling companions out of jail. One of the
few times she was thrown for a loss was during a dizzy spell
while visiting in Cuernavaca. "Bring me a pan, por favor," she
asked the Mexican housekeeper. The lady rushed Millie a loaf
of bread.

Millie and her mother are connected by an invisible 2-way
wire that permits of communication without recourse to the
Bell Telephone Co. "Mama's worried about something," she
will say. Hanging up on that psychic connection, she'll then pick
up a phone, call her mother 1,500 miles away, and sure enough—
the roof's leaking.

Millie went to work in the State Department in Washington
as a slip of a girl and there met an awkward youth who loitered
there as a misfile clerk and who dreamed wanly of making a
living at some other dodge, like writing. She said to this poor
soul one day, "Why don't you take a chance at newspaper work,
and if you flop, well, I'm working."

They were married on $90 she had saved, plus $100 the
fellow got from George E. Allen and George Riley, then Washington hotel men, for doing publicity on a pro tennis match
between Bill Tilden and Karel Kozeluh. They spent two extra
days on the Atlantic City end of their honeymoon. Her check
was late arriving.

Interviewed in the rubble of her Park Avenue apartment today, Millie said the only drawback to having a silver wedding anniversary is that there may be skeptics who'll no longer believe she's 39. I doubt that. She looked to her interviewer pretty much as she looked the first time he saw her, but better, and the thought occurred to him that if she were not already married he would ask her then and there.

I lived pretty well around our manse for a good two or three days after that appeared. Matter of truth, I've lived pretty well around our manse for a long time. Being married to Millie is anything but tedious. Human experience doesn't offer ready parallels, save to say that it is something like being a passenger on a roller coaster. On New Year's Eve.

Bob Considine

Swinging on a Coattail

The children are all grown and gone, and the big old country house begins to echo and rattle with the memories of the middle-aged parents left there alone. Over the anguished wails of the children, who want to hang on to the old homestead for sentimental reasons, the parents finally find a young couple with children who want to buy the house. Then they escape to a city apartment.

Yes, it happened to us too. And we discovered what everyone else in our shoes discovers—making the decision and selling the house is not the real problem. The real poser is clearing out of the storage closets, basement and attic the memorabilia of a lifetime.

The job might have been a little tougher for us because I tend to save every item that ever passes through my hands. Especially souvenirs from our travels. What use does anyone have, really, for an abacus, a dozen bottles of holy water, a 17th century card press?

Naturally, Bob was away on a newspaper assignment when it came time to sort everything out and pack. His sixth sense isn't limited to news stories, apparently. During any dreary household upheaval it's always been Pop goes, the weasel!

And so I sorted and packed alone—and it turned out to be fun. From discoveries in all of the trunks, boxes and closets I drew vivid flashbacks of good times with Bob, the children, our friends. . . .

An autographed picture of Gamal Nasser reminded me of a crazy, unreal tent party on the Sahara Desert . . . a crumpled Greek costume of a hysterical day at Delphi . . . an antique lace handkerchief of a wild stop at a Paris bordello . . . a Sèvres bon-bon dish brought back "Specs" O'Keefe, notorious Brink's robber . . . a newspaper clipping had me twisting again with J. Paul Getty. . . .

But come along while I go through it all, bit by bit.

Here's our yellowing marriage certificate. That's how it all began, this life spent swinging on the coattail of a world reporter.

Millie Considine

one

A Marriage Certificate

~§~ "Capital Limited" was the name of my train and coincidentally the state of my finances that day I left Kansas City for my first job in Washington, D.C.

I was scared and green the first day at work, in the Department of Communications and Records in the State Department. I was taken around and introduced to my co-workers, and out of the sea of strange faces only one stood out.

It wasn't the handsomest face I saw, but was the most interesting. It had a big nose, bright blue eyes, and seemed to radiate kindness and understanding. The name that went with the face was Bob Considine.

Little did I know that day would change the course of my life and lead to the most beautiful document I own — my marriage certificate.

Bob was a tennis champ, and it all began by his asking me to come watch him play in various matches. That led to lunches together, and from there we graduated to evening boat rides down the Potomac River. You may not believe this, but as two struggling — and frustrated — writers, we spent those beautiful evenings reading our latest masterpieces to each other. While I rowed the boat, Bob would read his most recent literary effort to me by flashlight. Then we'd change places — sometimes a precarious endeavor in the middle of the river — and he'd row while I read the poem or essay I'd ground out in my Government Hotel room the night before. In looking back it seems that his brain-children were always longer than mine!

That lasted for almost a year. Then one night, as we were leaving a George Washington University class in creative writing, Bob asked me to marry him! I'm still not sure what inspired me, but I haughtily answered, "I plan on marrying a writer, not a government clerk. You're good enough now, why don't you try for a newspaper job?"

The next day Bob asked for time off and went to Shirley Povich's office at the Washington *Post*. Not only did he get an interview, but he ended up with a weekly column. It was called "Speaking of Tennis," and paid a whole $5 a week. We'd always blow it all on a candlelight dinner at the Iron Gate Inn. That was the height of elegance to us.

The following summer Bob was given a full-time job as high school reporter for the *Post,* and they paid even less than the State Department. He was earning $31.50 a week to my $33. When he started pressing me to name a date for the wedding I accused him of marrying me for my money! Since neither of us had any to speak of, and since we only had two weeks off from work, we decided just to slip off to nearby Annapolis rather than going through all the fol-de-rol of a family wedding. We didn't breathe a word of our plans to anybody but Bill Shreve and Harriet Littler, the two friends we'd chosen to stand up for us.

Somehow Bob's sister Emily got wind of the plot and showed

up at St. Mary's Church holding her month-old baby. Assuming the baby was ours, and the wedding was way overdue, Father Clune decided to conduct the ceremony in record time. Only Bob delayed things by turning my $65 wedding ring around on my finger until he could see the little diamond chips on top. He still has 20-20 vision!

After the wedding we had lunch at Haddon Hall and then drove to Canada for our honeymoon. At each stop I'd wait in the car while Bob went inside to ask about the rates. We'd keep driving until we'd find places we could afford.

I don't remember where we stayed in Quebec, but I do recall we spent one whole afternoon in the lobby of the Chateau Frontenac Hotel writing notes to all our friends on the hotel stationery.

Our second-hand jalopy, a Ford with bright chintz lining (one of its former owners must have had material left over after making kitchen curtains), broke down in Atlantic City en route home. We had to wait there until my government check arrived to bail us out. At the time, we thought it was a lark. It makes me feel old to think of what my reaction would be now.

But even in those days life wasn't *all* poverty. By a stroke of great fortune we lived in splendor our first five years of marriage. George Riley, a friend of ours, was manager of the opulent old Wardman Park Hotel, which was then in a state of receivership and half empty. He let us live in an apartment with a bedroom, living room, kitchen and bath for $60 a month —just about what they charge each day for the same set-up now. Tea was served in the lobby every late afternoon, with finger sandwiches and cookies, and more often than not that was our dinner!

Bob's mother probably couldn't understand our extreme devotion — we went to see her two or three times a week — just before dinner. Naturally she'd always insist we stay for a bite. Her specialty was baked fresh pork, navy beans and Dutch apple cake, and I don't believe anything has ever tasted as good since.

(When I first met Bob's mother my immediate reaction was to hope Bob didn't inherit her fondness for cats. There were always loads of them leaping around the kitchen or lying in front of the stove. Later on I learned that because their little house was in the Swampoodle area of Washington, next to the railroad tracks, the cats were her only weapons against the rodents.)

Before we knew it, we had been married two years. Then Bob moved on from the *Post* to the Washington *Herald,* and was earning as much as we'd both been earning together before. Naturally I quit work.

By that time we were terribly frustrated that no baby had arrived on the scene, so when I quit work Mama and I took a 6,000 mile drive across the country with a dual purpose in mind: Mama was going to look up all her widely-scattered brothers and sisters, and I was going to search for a baby to adopt. We dismissed the world-famous Cradle in Chicago because we heard they only gave babies out for adoption to rich or famous families. Bob and I wanted a boy, and had his name all picked out — Robert Alan.

At one of our stops, Omaha, our hostess told us there was a good orphanage in town. I was in the car and on my way almost before she finished the sentence.

"Darling, I've found Robert Alan," I wrote Bob that night, "and believe it or not his name actually *is* Robert Alan. I went to an orphanage here in Omaha, and the nun walked me out into the garden where the babies were playing under a tree. A beautiful little blond, blue-eyed boy two years old turned around and saw us and ran straight to me and held out his arms. I was so thrilled I thought I'd die. Then when the nun told me his name was Robert Alan I knew this was fate. 'He's mine,' I said to the nun. She told me to come back tomorrow morning to make the arrangements. Isn't it wonderful I found him the very first place I looked?"

The next day I sent Bob a telegram. "Darling, I found Robert Alan yesterday but lost him today. A family who saw him a few days ago and were thinking it over went to the orphanage and picked him up this morning. Disregard letter enroute."

I was so disheartened by that experience I discontinued the search during my trip with Mama. After I returned to Washington Bob and I checked the orphanages within the area, but with no luck.

A couple of years later we became friendly with George Preston Marshall, who owned the Redskins football team, and his wife Corinne Griffith. Corinne told us about a place in New York where she had adopted her two children and where Helen Hayes had adopted her son. I immediately contacted the adoption society, and we had a long correspondence that lasted six months — mostly a check-up on our background and fitness as would-be parents. They impressed upon us that it was their policy to find a baby with as nearly as possible the same religious and intellectual background as ours, and that would take time.

By the time they'd found a baby they considered suitable, we were in the midst of a big leap from Washington to New York. Bob finally got what he wanted most — a job on a New York newspaper, the New York *American*. The moment we arrived in New York we went to see the little boy they had chosen for us, and that chubby, smiling, brown-eyed baby, nine months old, became ours in every sense of the word. Mike was the only name for that funny little puss, and so he became Michael Riley Considine. That "Riley" was the least we could do for George Riley, our Wardman Park benefactor.

To me, nothing beats a family for making a woman happy. But sometimes as Mike grew older and I saw him dancing and playing alone in front of a mirror I'd creep into the bedroom and cry. I couldn't seem to produce a little brother or sister for him. Just as I was beginning to get really morbid and berating myself for being a sterile, worthless woman, the second miracle happened. What I thought was an ulcer turned out to be Barry, our firstborn.

Bob and I decided that with our family increasing, we should move to the country so Mike and the coming baby could have sun and air. Our idea of the country at that time was Forest Hills. "Country living just fifteen minutes from the city by subway," the ads said.

The house we found was charming — Dutch Colonial with a split front door and fireplaces in almost every room. Immersed in the spirit of country living we even acquired a big red Irish setter whose name happened to be "Irish." What else do you need to settle down happily to country life?

Oh, there were a few problems. There was that nice woman we hired to take care of Mike and the house, for example. On her second day while she was walking Irish on his heavy leash, Irish spotted a cat across the street. He took off and so did she. The result was a broken collarbone. Irish seemed to prefer the local dog pound to us, and that's where he'd run away to at least once a day. We knew where to look for him, but it did get to be a bore.

And just as I was beginning to adjust to the bats and birds who decided our fireplaces made a snug harbor, a neighbor came to see me for the first time. As we were sipping our tea, she asked if we didn't feel at all funny living in the house.

"Not at all," I answered quite truthfully.

"You don't have any qualms about going into that room where the old man hung himself?"

"*What* old man — *what* room?"

"Oh, I thought somebody must have told you. That's why the last family moved out. The old man got so upset over the bats and rats and everything he hung himself."

The Warwick Hotel, where we moved the next day, proved a relaxing place to finish out my confinement. Mama took Mike back to Kansas City with her for the few remaining months until the new baby arrived. We had a voluminous correspondence with the owner of the Forest Hills house, but were still stuck with paying the rent on it for the six months it took us to find another sucker to take it over.

As it happened, Mike needed his tonsils out at the same time I went to the hospital to have Barry. Bob flew to Kansas City to bring Mike to Babies Hospital, and I had Barry in adjoining Harkness Pavilion.

When Mike and I were both able to sit up in wheel chairs (in those days they didn't get new mothers up to walk the first day), our respective nurses took us out into the garden so we could see each other and have a ride together. As we were being wheeled down an incline my nurse somehow lost her grip on my wheel chair (frankly I never did think she liked me much) and I went hurtling down the hill so fast I had to leap out and start running with my robe flying out behind me. It meant two more days in bed for me, and a big, beautiful laugh for Mike.

With two boys, I felt we had a real family, and then when

Barry was nine months old, Mrs. Bugs Baer came to visit me. I became ill during her call and two days later I read in Ed Sullivan's column: "Are the Bob Considines infanticipating again?" That's how I found out about Dennis!

two

Papa's Drugstore

◈ I hadn't seen that stiff, brownish picture of Papa standing on front of his drugstore for years. Osage, Oklahoma, of all places. I was only six years old at the time, but I remember the day it was taken.

I was hiding behind the cigar store Indian while the photographer fiddled around under the black hood on his big box camera, set on a tripod. He'd told us kids to stay out of the way. My brother Raymond was peeking around the corner of the store, and my oldest brother Leonard was inside peering out through the big bottles of blue liquid that for some unaccountable reason were always the window dressing of drugstores in those days. Mama was standing by with a comb in case the wind ruffled Papa's neatly combed black hair, parted in the middle. Taking pictures was a big deal then.

Whenever I think of my childhood my immediate association is with drugstores. By the time I was twelve, we had lived and had drugstores in at least twelve different towns — the first eleven in Oklahoma and finally, Kansas City. I never knew whether

Papa was one jump ahead of the sheriff or just had the wander-lust I inherited. Changing schools and friends so often was as tough on us kids as the constant packing and unpacking was on Mama. At least we were never bored.

We usually lived in an apartment at the back of or over the store, and since Mama helped Papa in the store, we all spent most of our waking hours there. I'd do my homework at a back table, and if it was busy I'd help out. Even now I never get a whiff of a prescription counter or a soda fountain without thinking of Papa.

Our busiest days in our Osage store were Saturdays. On Friday Papa would stock up heavily on hair tonic, which in those days had a high alcoholic content. On Saturday morning the Indians from the nearby reservation, dressed in blankets and feathers, would start trooping into the store. By early afternoon the hair tonic shelf would be bare and the street would be full of drunk Indians!

During slack times we'd go to our living room at the back of the store and play the player piano or Mama would entertain us with stories of her escapades involving Indians in the early days of Oklahoma before it became a state. Most of my bad dreams concerned the Indian who tried to kidnap Mama one day. She had always been unusually pretty, with big china-blue eyes, chestnut hair, and a lovely figure. I remember how all the sales-men who used to come into the store did their best to make time with her. They'd have one stock phrase when they saw me. They'd look at Mama, and then me again, and say "What a pity she looks like J.J. instead of you." Papa wasn't at all bad-looking, but Mama was definitely the one I preferred to resemble.

From what I was told of their Civil War experiences, I was

always more proud of my maternal grandfather than of my paternal one. Mama's father, who was born in Dublin, came to America when he was seventeen, learned to be a doctor in Louisiana, and then braved the wilds of Oklahoma to practice. He fought on the side of the South, but once when he knew one of his own babies was due he went AWOL, beat it home to deliver the baby, and then went back to war. But I must admit that Papa's father seemed more clever. During the Civil War he hired a man to fight in his place. The war for him meant sitting on his front porch smoking a pipe and visiting with his neighbors.

I guess Papa must have felt a little guilty about his father. I remember during World War II, while we were walking Barry in Central Park, we saw a young man sprawled on a park bench reading a book. "What a dirty slacker," Papa said indignantly, "sitting there reading a book when he ought to be off fighting."

When we came abreast of the young man we saw that the book was Bob's *Thirty Seconds Over Tokyo* about Captain Lawson and the Doolittle Raid. "Poor son of a bitch probably has heart trouble," said Papa.

Our store burned down one Sunday while we were out having a drive in our horse and buggy. The clerk left in charge saved only one thing. Instead of grabbing the prescriptions or the money in the cash register, he yanked the telephone off the wall and ran out.

It was through our drugstores that I learned the facts of life. If a young man came into the store and seemed terribly embarrassed when I started to wait on him, I soon learned to call Papa. Sure enough he'd come and head straight for the drawer of little tin boxes. I wondered why buying white balloons would embarrass anyone until my brother Raymond set me straight. At least he gave me enough of a teaser so that Mama had to go ahead and tell me the rest.

Lydia Pinkham used to advertise "a baby in every bottle," and I used to hold the bottles up against the light to see if I could discern even the seed of a baby. I drank a glass full of the nasty stuff once and then told Mama I was going to get a baby. She didn't seem unduly concerned. But then I was only ten years old.

Our drugstores deprived me of Santa Claus. We were allowed to look over the Christmas stock of toys and pick out what we wanted put aside for our presents. Most of my friends thought that was a distinct advantage, but I didn't. I wanted to be surprised. Mama and Papa always worked past midnight on Christmas Eve making last-minute sales, so they never had time to bother with a tree. Our presents were piled on chairs. Each of us had a special chair staked out. There were always a few surprises that Mama had secretly made for us, knitted sweaters and helmets for the boys, and dresses and new doll clothes for me. My best Christmas was the time I found on my chair the beautiful bonnet I'd spotted in a store window in Kansas City. It was black velvet and inside the brim was fluted pink satin.

When I first saw it in the window about a month before Christmas, I dragged Mama downtown to show it to her. We both drooled over it, but of course it was out of the question. It cost $25. I wanted it more than I'd ever wanted anything in my life before — or since — but I never dreamed I'd actually get it. As soon as I saw it Christmas morning, I put it on. When Mama tried to straighten the brim for me, I screeched, as only a thoughtless child can, "Don't touch it. You might ruin it."

It wasn't until a month later that I was rummaging through

Mama's sewing machine drawers for a button and found the little scraps of black velvet and pink satin that let me know she had *made* the hat for me herself. She had to admit she'd gone down and studied the hat in the window, gotten the materials, and carefully copied it for me at night when I was asleep. She'd even explained the situation to a salesgirl in the hat department and conned the girl into giving her an empty hatbox with the store's name on the outside.

I was flooded with shame, remembering I'd told Mama not to touch the hat. I also loved her more than ever.

Romance came to me through the drugstores too. When I was six years old I fell in love with Oscar Alexander, a much older man. He was nine and made deliveries for Papa. I really think it was sympathy more than love — Oscar was cross-eyed and all the other little girls made fun of him.

A train stopped in Osage once a day, and one day Oscar and I decided to elope on it. I took along a little suitcase containing Daisy, my favorite doll, and her clothes. All Oscar took was a Sears Roebuck catalogue from which to select our furniture. The elopement was foiled as soon as we sat down on the train. The conductor recognized me and held up the train while he marched me by the ear back to Papa's store.

My next brush with love came a couple of years later after we'd moved to Blackwell, Oklahoma. I fell for Allen Fey, whose father owned the butcher shop near our drugstore. Allen had a Buster Brown bob and I thought he was beautiful. One day I dressed up in one of Mama's lace curtains and one of the neighborhood kids performed a mock marriage between Allen and me. After that we assiduously cleaned out the tool shack in our back yard, furnished it with broken-down furniture from the basement, and for quite a spell played house all day. It couldn't have been too serious, though, because we alternated being papa and mama.

As I grew older I discovered the drugstore helped immeasurably toward bolstering my popularity. When my friends and I got home from school we'd all go behind the soda fountain and concoct the most marvelous delicacies. No plain old banana splits for us! We'd pile on pineapple, fudge, cherries, nuts, marshmallow, whipped cream, butterscotch, and sometimes a squirt of Coca-Cola or root beer syrup. I had more friends than anyone else in school.

There always seemed to be a neighborhood movie theatre near our drugstores, and no matter how bad business might be during an evening, Papa would always wait until the last show let out to catch a few stragglers at the soda fountain before closing up. To fill the void until closing time, I'd always slip into the last showing of the movie, alone. I had a whole private world of excitement, travel, beautiful clothes and romance. My favorite star was Gloria Swanson, and if anyone had told me then I would one day travel through Europe with her, I would have said he was nuts.

three

Deed to a House

✍⟨§⟩❧ Whenever I think of that trip with Gloria, my next thought is of the big old house in Allenhurst that we sold. We bought it, unexpectedly, the summer of 1954, after several happy, irresponsible summers renting furnished homes. We'd had occasional (*very* occasional) spurts of wanting a "home of our own," but until that summer they'd go away as rapidly as they came. To me, both the house and my trip seem a package deal.

At the time, I was writing a monthly column about celebrities, travel, society and all that for *DIPLOMAT* Magazine. I took the job mainly so I could be included in the worldwide press junkets to which Bob was constantly being invited. Interesting material being practically (what do I mean *practically!*) nonexistent in Allenhurst (where we had a summer rental), I was casting around for ideas for the column when I got a call from Earl Blackwell that solved the problem. He suggested I join him and Gloria Swanson in Monte Carlo for a few soirées, after which we'd go to Venice where Earl was planning to give "the party of

the year" in a Venetian palace. Earl owns an organization called
"Celebrity Service," and there's always column material around
him — his *business* is celebrities and parties. And so with my
family in the super-capable hands of our housekeeper Anny
Haller, who came to us when the boys were babies, I decided to
go along with Earl and Gloria.

Just a few days before I was to leave, our neighbors the Meehans asked us to look at a house they were thinking of buying.
It was the showplace of the whole town (the whole town being
five blocks square), and since we'd long been curious to see the
inside of the place we gladly went along.

Once they got us inside, the Meehans told us they'd decided
the house was too big for them ("What would we do with eight
bedrooms!") and suggested *we* buy it. While we were inspect-
ing the house the Meehans subtly threw in little comments such
as "very low taxes . . . saves all the trouble of moving everything back and forth to New York every spring and fall . . .
it's a joy to own your own home . . . imagine picking flowers
for the house out of your own yard . . . much cheaper than
renting in the long run . . . you can grow your own vegetables
in case of war. . . ."

The house was for sale completely furnished, and despite some
of the garish drapes, wallpaper and decor, we all loved it. We
each picked out our own rooms mentally. We could see ourselves
having steak-fries at the enormous stone barbecue in the back
yard (Bob eyed that with particular relish) or leisurely breakfasts on the screened-in side porch. We were already decorating
the tall cedar trees in the side yard with Christmas lights.

We talked of little else during the next few days, the kids with
great enthusiasm, Bob and I with restraint. We decided that I
was to go ahead to Europe and Bob, who was substituting for

Walter Winchell on his show that summer, would try to work something out. There was still a very big *IF* about the whole thing.

Gloria and Earl were already in Monte Carlo when I arrived. I called Gloria's suite at the Hotel de Paris and she told me to come up. When I walked in, Earl, very red-faced, was screaming into the telephone. He was saying "Milan, Ischia, Corsica, Helvetia, Elba, Lugano, Lisbon, Egypt . . . pause, Amalfi, Madrid, Orbotello and Naples." I didn't know whether he was playing "geography" or outlining a trip.

"We're trying to call my daughter in Paris," Gloria explained. "The operator can't seem to understand a simple name like Michelle Amon."

It's very true that the French phone operators can better understand letters the way Americans say them if they're fitted to a familiar city or word. I told Gloria about the difficulty I had one time in Paris when I was trying to call a friend whose phone number was MA-7834. I simply could not make the operator understand that exchange, MA. The only familiar French words I could think of at that moment came out quite automatically. I said "M A, comme merde alors." I got the number immediately. Also a giggle every time I picked up the phone after that.

We spent several delightful days on the Riviera, which included lunch with Fiat king Gianni Agnelli at his magnificent estate, La Leopolda, an afternoon with Aly Khan and Bettina at L'Horizon in Golfe Juan, and endless parties. My column was sizzling.

Our funniest experience was one I couldn't use for the magazine. One day we drove over to Cap Ferrat to have luncheon with a famous American hostess. The minute we walked in, she said, "Gloria, why don't you have those lines around your eyes taken

care of? Millie, why do you keep that disgusting big bosom?"
Before Gloria could fight for her lines, and me for my bosom,
our hostess started pointing out the charms she'd acquired
through plastic surgery.

"The scars around my eyes still show a little because I just had
them redone in England two weeks ago, but look at my eyes —
not a line." She was right. Not a line. But her eyes had a staring,
almost frightened look, and the skin was so smooth and stretched
over her face it looked completely expressionless, like a mask.
Also she could barely smile.

Then she turned her attention to my problem. "You know you
don't *have* to be stuck with that big bosom. You can have an
operation that will make you flat as a boy and never have to
wear a brassiere. Look at me." With that she yanked off her
blouse and sure enough she was almost as flat as a boy. There
was an added feature too — under each breast was a crisscrossed
scar that looked like a miniature railroad track. It seemed to me
any close pal who wasn't scared off by the flat bosom in the first
place would certainly be scared off by those tracks.

Gloria and I could hardly wait to escape with our favorite
features intact. We laughed until we were weak.

When it came time for Earl to go to Venice to prepare for his
party, Gloria and I decided on the spur of the moment that we
wanted to see Portofino before joining him.

The little train that runs along the Riviera is the bête noire of
the idle rich whose rest it disturbs night and day with its huffing,
puffing and shrill whistle. It's fun to travel on, though. It runs
quite close to the houses along the way, and once we got into
Italy the whole mood changed. Instead of disgruntled French
people glaring at us, we saw happy, laughing Italians leaning
out of their windows, which in some cases were almost flush

with the train. They all recognized Gloria and yelled and waved to her. She hadn't made a movie in a long time, but Gloria is recognizable all over the world because of her unique face. There have been others who resembled Garbo, Dietrich, Crawford, and other old-time movie queens, but I've never seen anybody who even remotely looked like Gloria, least of all her daughters Gloria and Michelle.

She's the most fascinating woman I've ever met. Never for a moment has she stopped being a movie queen. She's always "on." You'd never catch her on the street or in a grocery store in dungarees and tennis shoes, or without makeup and hair out of place. Her sleek brown hair would be neatly combed, and the eye makeup she wears to accentuate her magnetic eyes would be on. Her tiny, slim figure would be encased in a chic black dress, and she'd probably have on a leopard stole. Gloria favors leopard and uses it profusely in her Fifth Avenue apartment as a bed cover on her low, Japanese-style bed, as pillows and as floor coverings.

A five-foot bundle of dynamic energy, Gloria never slows down. She designs clothes, and travels all over the world promoting them, paints and sculpts well, takes singing lessons, and reads scripts constantly.

Gloria attributes her energy to her eating habits, which are strict and unusual. She eats nothing but organically-fertilized food — even the meat has to be from animals that were fed organically. Her bread is baked at home from a special kind of whole wheat. Once while driving from California to New York she subsisted on nuts and fruit. "Whenever we wanted to stop to eat they had nothing but those awful hamburgers and malted milks!" (The very things that make *me* drool!)

Sometimes it's a pain in the neck to go to restaurants with

Gloria. Most waiters don't seem to understand the value of organically-fertilized food, or sometimes even what it *is*. Gloria doesn't think it's funny when I say "I'd rather have chemicals on my food than manure."

Gloria is so steamed up against the use of chemicals in growing food she keeps writing letters to congressmen and senators trying to get them to pass a law forbidding it. She's equally vehement on the value of Krebiozen for cancer. She's all for Krebiozen, and her pet hate is the American Medical Association for not accepting it. On one of my radio interview shows she got a bit too vehement about it and we were cut off the air!

Gloria once had a long-playing gentleman friend about her age from whom she was inseparable. They went together to Dr. Niehans' famous clinic in Switzerland for the shots of unborn lamb that are supposed to make the recipients youthful and healthy. The shots worked so well, Gloria and her friend dropped each other and both started going out with much younger people. Otherwise I saw no change whatever in Gloria after the shots. She always did look younger than her age and could easily lie about it but never does. She admits to being born March 27, 1899. That admission alone makes her unique. Her mother is in her mid-eighties and is just about as sprightly and energetic as Gloria.

Anyway, we hadn't bothered to make reservations in Portofino, and were amazed when we arrived to discover we couldn't get even one hotel room there. We were dismayed, to say the least. We loved Portofino. It's one of the most picturesque places in the world. The whole life of the town centers around the small rounded port where the yachts and fishing boats anchor. The sidewalk cafés overflow with gay, happy customers. The little shops are colorful, with women sitting outside working on native handicrafts.

Someone suggested we try to get accommodations at nearby Santa Marguerita. Even there the situation was tight, but we finally managed to get one small room for the two of us in a tiny waterfront hotel. I thought Gloria would be disgruntled, as it was a far cry from the huge suite she'd had at the Hotel de Paris. On the contrary she was enchanted. "But these are the real Italians *here*," she happily enthused. "Look at all these beautiful Italian children running around . . . look at the face on that old man selling fruit in the street . . . isn't it marvelous!"

As soon as we'd unpacked, and I'd wired Bob where I was, Gloria and I went out into the village on a shopping expedition. It's amazing what good buys you can find. The greatest skirts, blouses, beaded jackets and bibelots for so little money. Soon, though, we had to give up, because of the marvelously large entourage of Swanson fans that accumulated.

That night we went to a cocktail party on Sam Spiegel's yacht, followed by a hilarious dinner at a waterfront restaurant. By now any thought of buying a house in Allenhurst, New Jersey, was crowded far to the back of my mind. Back at the hotel, I told Gloria I hoped I wouldn't disturb her sleep as I was a very light sleeper and spent half the night smoking cigarettes or reading. The next thing I knew she was shaking me, light was streaming in the windows, and a waiter was carrying out Gloria's breakfast dishes.

"Too bad you sleep so lightly, kid," she said, "you didn't even hear me order or eat my breakfast — there's a telegram."

The telegram said: "I've bought the house come on home and help move in I love you Bob."

So, Gloria went to Venice and I went to Allenhurst, New Jersey. Very simple.

I've often thought of those helpful little comments of the Meehans . . . "imagine picking flowers out of the yard, you can grow your own vegetables . . . cheaper than renting in the long run." Ha!

I picked the flowers from the yard all right. Between doctor bills for bee stings, the seeds, and the gardener's $75 a month I figure each bouquet only costs $5, or about $2 more than the same bouquet would have cost at Jameson's Florist around the corner. And then there was the vegetable garden out by the garage. Each cherry tomato couldn't have cost us more than a dollar!

By the time we paid for the house, paid the taxes, painted the house every few years at $2,000 a whack, fixed up the basement, papered and repapered the rooms, had a new electrical system installed to take care of the air conditioners, bought the air conditioners, bought new awnings twice, put in new linoleum and rugs, changed the draperies, installed a fire alarm system, kept an electrical repair man, a handyman, a furnace repair man and an awning-upkeep man in business for eleven years, we figure we only spent as much as we'd have paid out renting summer houses for fifty years.

There's no denying it though, there is a certain smug satisfaction in "owning your own home." It was great at Thanksgiving and Christmas with our family and friends gathered around the huge table in the Delft dining room with an enormous turkey on it ready for Bob to carve. After the frantic pace of cities and resorts, a solid roomy house feels like an old shoe. You can be sociable rather than social. Only once did I try to impress some society-type guests who drove out for dinner. It was a flop. I decided our dear old cook Rosie might not be sufficiently elegant to serve the dinner, so I called an employment agency in New York to send out a high-class butler for the occasion. I might have been able to convince the guests he was part of our regular staff, but not Mimi, our dog. When our guests heard we had a poodle, they volunteered that they were poodle lovers and asked to see her. I explained I had her shut up in a bathroom because she wasn't at all friendly with strangers — in fact, she bit them. Just as our fancy strange butler started to serve the jellied consommé, Mimi somehow escaped and came bounding into the dining room. She had one look at the butler and took a flying leap at the seat of his pants. The jig was up.

In our home the bar doubles as a music room. We'd have endless sessions with Barry playing the piano, Debbie and Dennis the guitar, and me the bongo drums. Not a motherly instrument, I agree, but the only one I'd mastered. It was fun with Toots Shor, Billy Reed and Tony deMarco doing a soft-shoe dance, with Bob, the Tony Storys and Walter Kiebach standing around the bar singing off key, but loudly.

The hours and hours we spent showing home movies and the almost continuous badminton, croquet, Ping-Pong or card games were to me the most. And for a while we had that pleasant, secure feeling that we'd always have a home — even if Bob lost his job. Eventually, of course, we realized that with Bob not working we couldn't afford to stay in the house for even a month.

The house in Allenhurst, filled with four growing, active kids, was a far cry from the first summer home we rented in Rye, New York, when Mike was six and Barry was just born.

four

A Clipping from "Believe It Or Not"

❧ That was quite a summer we had in Rye, New York. One of our neighbors was Robert L. Ripley. What made Ripley particularly endearing to me, I must confess, was that he used an anecdote I gave him in the Kansas City *Star*. It was a story about Mama and Buddy, her tiny Boston bulldog. Buddy would spend all of his time in the drugstore with us, and one trick that Mama taught him became a real drawing card for the store. He'd sit up and beg for a penny, then run and hide it in his sleeping basket. He accumulated quite a horde. Whenever Buddy felt like having a dish of ice cream he'd pick up one of the pennies in his mouth, run over to Mama, and drop the penny at her feet. She'd put the penny in the cash register and let any customer wait while she gave Buddy his dish of ice cream. She was as excited as I was when the item appeared in the *Star*.

While I was in Harkness Pavilion having Barry, Bob scouted around and found a summer rental house in Rye. We went straight from the hospital to our new temporary home. The

house was on Mamaroneck Lane, facing a lake, in a secluded little area that might have been a world apart.

That summer Ripley was living on a small island he called
Bion (Believe It Or Not) in the middle of the lake. Actually
we had quite a few exceptional neighbors. Ethel Barrymore lived
in the first house on the road and Ezio Pinza in the last one.
Every time I wheeled Barry down the road in his baby-carriage
I seemed to encounter Pinza giving *his* baby a buggy ride. Not
being an opera buff, I wasn't impressed with Pinza as an opera
star, but of course was interested in him as the father of another
baby. Until he pinched me the first time. Later, on trips to
Rome, I was to learn fanny-pinching comes quite naturally to
Italians and means nothing. But at the time I was naive enough
to be disconcerted and started wheeling Barry in a different
direction after the second or third pinch. Of course I could have
kicked myself a couple of years later when I sighed over him
as the hero of "South Pacific"! That turned out to be my closest
contact with the Metropolitan Opera.

Since Ripley and Bob both worked for Hearst, we all became
quite friendly and we were invited over to Bion for cocktails
almost daily. We could reach his house either by rowing over in
a boat or walking over an arched Chinese bridge that seemed
about to collapse.

Ripley was stranger than any of the people he put in his
cartoons, and so was his ménage. The house itself was generally
Oriental in motif, but there was a little of every other type of
decor as well. A huge totem pole dominated the lawn, at the
foot of which was a well-tended dog cemetery where the departed
canines of Ripley and his friends lay in splendor. They were surmounted by sweet little tombstones bearing the dogs' names.

The house had thirty-odd rooms. Very odd. All were filled

with mementos from Ripley's travels in search of the unusual. I sympathized with his housekeeper who had to dust it all. She was the only one allowed to touch anything — not that anybody else particularly wanted to.

The bar was overpowered by a nine-foot ossified whale's penis hung across the top of the room. Conversely enough, there were hundreds of temple bells strung around the barroom which Ripley rang to summon his strange household to cocktails.

The real grotesqueries that Ripley had collected were kept in the basement — pictures of horribly malformed people, shrunken heads and other "souvenirs." An Ecuadorian once shipped a shrunken head to Ripley with a covering note that read "Please take care of this, I think it is one of my relatives." Sometimes when Ripley was showing guests through the basement he'd pick up a head and kiss it affectionately.

I particularly remember a ghastly picture of an entire African family of ten whose legs all ended in points just below their knees, and another picture of a man whose privates were so swollen with elephantiasis he had to carry them in a wheelbarrow.

Even more gruesome to me than the horrors in the basement, though, was a wooden statue standing at the head of the stairs. It was carved by a Japanese artist just before he committed suicide. He had pulled off his own fingernails and toenails and put them on the statue, put his own teeth into it, and apparently scalped himself and put his own hair on it. I never did get up enough nerve to look under the skirt of the statue.

There were praying benches with lighted votive candles and religious statues all about on the second-floor landing, but these were almost overwhelmed by erotic paintings of women with snakes wound around them. The painting that dominated the second floor, though, was anything but erotic. It depicted a sweet Russian wedding and was so large it filled one whole wall. This was Ripley's pride and joy and he gave small replicas of it to all his friends.

That's only part of Ripley's sentimental side. The door to his bedroom was formerly the front door of the little house where he was born in Santa Rosa, California. He bought the whole house just to get the door.

But, as I said, the atmosphere at Bion was decidedly Oriental. I think this dates back to Ripley's first job as a cartoonist in San Francisco. He spent most of his leisure time in Chinatown, in dim little restaurants, listening to stories of the Orient told by old men in long gowns, wearing queues, and smoking slender reed pipes.

Love of the Orient extended to Ripley's ménage. The more or less permanent guests included a lovely little Japanese girl I'll call Haruko, and a brilliantly intellectual Chinese girl. There was also a regular of undetermined age who was rumored to be Ripley's first sweetheart, a secretary and several other females. Even more came over weekends. We were given to understand that once Ripley took an interest in a girl there was a bond between them forever after — no matter what.

We were told an imaginative tale about a woman Ripley married when he was young. Some time after they were divorced, the wife was supposed to have gone to Ripley and asked him to sign a paper saying he was a heathen and they'd had no religious ceremony. Although not knowing why, Ripley did so. A few years later Ripley had an appointment to interview a sheik at his tent in the Sahara, and seated next to the sheik was a woman he introduced as his wife. She was partly veiled, but even so, Ripley thought she bore a remarkable resemblance to his own former wife. Nothing was said about it at the time. That night a bearer brought a note to Ripley's hotel which said "You know I will always love you, LeRoy." His former wife was the only one who had ever called him by his middle name.

Togetherness seemed to prevail at Bion. It was rumored they all took sunbaths, sauna baths, steambaths and massages en masse, along with Ripley. I only know of one occasion when jealousy erupted, and that was during a Christmas dinner. Two of the girls had words and ended up digging into the turkey's rear and throwing fistsful of chestnut dressing at each other across the table. Ordinarily the harem got along very well, and even went shopping together for bolts of material to be made into dresses.

For cocktail parties the girls all wore native dress, which meant largely Oriental, but Ripley managed to have a different getup on each time. One day it would the ballet-type costume of a Greek *Evzoné,* next day it would be Chinese robes, next day a Tibetan outfit, and some days we didn't even recognize what the costume was supposed to represent.

Little Haruko was my favorite of the harem. She was small-boned and delicate, with porcelain-like skin and black hair worn to her shoulders, with thick bangs across her forehead. She looked like every Japanese doll you've ever seen. The native dress with its colorful obi that she always wore suited her perfectly.

Haruko seemed fascinated by my new baby, and started showing up at our house every four hours to watch me nurse him. She'd row over wearing a huge straw hat and carrying an armful of flowers, and would just sit quietly and watch while I fed Barry.

Finally one day I said, "Haruko, I can understand why Ripley might enjoy this, but why on earth do *you?*" Then she told me she had once been married to a Chinese boy by whom she had a baby that she too nursed, but the baby died. Watching me, she said, brought back happy memories.

One day Ripley gave a barbecue party on his lawn, and after a while I noticed Haruko wasn't around. The housekeeper told me Ripley was angry at Haruko because he'd caught her playing cards with Nick Kenny, and had banished her to her room. The housekeeper suggested I go on up to see her if I wanted to.

Finding Haruko's room in that tremendous house was no mean feat, but I managed by following the sound of sobbing. She brightened up when I appeared, and flitted about showing me the authentic opium bed where she slept, several statues whose hands, heads, arms and various other appendages bobbed up and down when touched, and a glass case containing several beautiful ivory boxes. I admired them all, but when I picked up the prettiest one to examine it closely, Haruko said, "That is where I keep my baby's ashes." When I quickly replaced the box on the shelf, Haruko said, "Oh don't worry, they aren't there now. When he's mad at me he hides them."

Ripley finally lost Haruko, as well as one of the other girls from the harem. Beyond the house on Long Island Sound where Ripley had a private beach, he kept his Chinese junk, "Mon Lei." Once during a cruise on the inland waterways to Florida, Ripley was called away on business. While he was gone, the two girls ran off and married two of the crew members.

The "Mon Lei" had originally been built for a Chinese warlord, but was confiscated and brought to San Francisco. She ended up in a Baltimore shipyard where Ripley found and bought her for $7500. He spent a small fortune modernizing the vessel, installing powerful diesel engines, showers, Beautyrest mattresses and ship-to-shore radio-telephones, yet leaned over backward to retain the flavor of a genuine Foochow fishing junk. Despite the diesel power, Ripley insisted on having the patched sails up at all times for effect. To conform to the old Chinese belief that a boat moves only because there is a dragon inside of it, Ripley painted the diesels into the likeness of traditional Chinese dragons with eyes, teeth and whiskers.

A butterfly of good luck was painted on the bow, and eyes were painted on each side to keep up another old Chinese tradition, "No got eyes, no can see; no can see, no can walk." The original colors of all Foochow fishing boats, a mixture of red, blue, white and various other hues was retained on the hull, spiked up with apt Chinese symbols here and there.

Ripley put Oriental paintings, carvings, teak furniture and opium beds in the cabin. Over the bed in the master stateroom was a large Chinese symbol that meant "I wish you one thousand lays." Also on the junk were a god of happiness, a colorful beaded prayer wheel, a statue of the many-armed Buddha of Benevolence and bells on the four corners of the pagoda pilothouse that were sounded each time the "Mon Lei" sailed, to ward off evil spirits. The final non-Chinese touches were a gold-plated anchor and red nylon ropes.

Obviously the "Mon Lei" attracted a good deal of attention. One day during one of our cruises in the Sound, Ripley was standing on a deck in a full mandarin costume, holding a long execution sword when a small cabin cruiser edged up and Ripley noticed that the middle-aged occupants were completely nude. Apparently they were sunbathing.

"Exhibitionists!" he exclaimed disdainfully.

It was inevitable that Ripley's unorthodoxy made him the subject of all kinds of wild rumors. One neighbor told us Ripley had a Chinese cook who was so terrified of a thirty-foot python

Ripley kept as a pet that he'd hanged himself out the kitchen window. Another story was that he'd had all his teeth extracted and pig's teeth put in their place.

Whether the stories are true or not, they do add to the Ripley exotica. With his sense of humor, I'm even inclined to suspect he perpetrated the rumors himself.

Many years after we were Ripley's neighbors, Bob wrote a book about him. I can't beat his description of Ripley's dual nature: "A living paradox, Ripley owned the most expensive foreign cars but never summoned up enough courage to drive; he consumed enormous quantities of liquor and may have set a record for romantic dalliance, but considered smoking and card-playing evil and would have nothing to do with them. He was, to his friends, the very personification of shyness, but no contemporary matched him in flamboyance or in seeking notoriety."

As far as we could see, Ripley led a rather normal life except for his unusual surroundings and unorthodox household. We never heard the nocturnal screams a few of his other neighbors said they heard. They certainly never came during those periods we were awake for the 10 P.M., 2 A.M. and 6 A.M. feedings of the baby.

And I can't think of anything more normal than his favorite pastime — the movies. On those nights when Ripley and his houseguests went, we'd have a barbecue in our yard. Bob was in the throes of being the domesticated man of the house. We had one of those little barbecues on wheels, and for a couple of hours at sunset, Bob would get the charcoal at what he considered the right temperature. He'd stand guard over the steaks or chops while they cooked, and mix up his own special barbecue sauce of which he was very proud. I don't mind divulging the secret

recipe. Just heat a mixture of ketchup and chili sauce in a sauce-
pan.

It was sort of a lonely job for Bob because the smoke and
mosquitoes drove the rest of us away.

We'd usually start eating on the lawn by the lake, but almost
invariably would end up indoors because of mosquitoes or rain
squalls. It took all evening, but what else was there to do when
Ripley was at the movies?

five

The Group

~§~ What a picture! But then again, what a group we were. I guess every woman has a "group." Mine ostensibly met for card games and luncheons, but not really. I know we also welcomed the opportunity to show off our new clothes and exchange the latest gossip.

Like most "groups," we made a concentrated effort to dress as much alike as possible, and then as good narcissists we'd exclaim over each other's appearance. I see from this old photo that we all have on similar crazy hats with veils, feathers and flowers, and the Adrian suits with exaggerated shoulders that were then in vogue. The only furs worn were silver foxes. I bet we also had on ankle-strap shoes and gold anklets.

The "girls" were Hope Hampton, Louise (Mrs. Bugs) Baer, Sylvia (Mrs. Ed) Sullivan, Rose (Mrs. Walter) Shirley, Charlene (Mrs. David) Marx, Eve Sully (of the Block and Sully vaudeville team), Sugar Smullion, Frances Moody, Cherry Thirkield (who later became the famous painter, Huldah) and a few others who joined us irregularly.

We'd meet once a week to have lunch and play gin rummy, either at someone's apartment or at the Stork Club. At the Stork, we'd go upstairs to a private room after lunch and half the girls would line up on one side of the table as a team against the girls lined up on the other side.

It's good we didn't play for much money (I think a tenth of a cent a point was our stakes), because the games were more conversation than anything else.

"Why do you carry a gold cigarette case when you don't smoke?" someone would ask Hope. Every game along the table would stop.

"To keep gum and aspirin in," she explained. "Besides it looks nice in the bag."

Two seconds later someone would say, "Where did you get that darling hat, Rose?"

No action, until we dissected not only Rose's hat, but every other hat in the room.

"How's your new maid working out, Millie?" would be good for a ten-minute discussion of domestic help problems.

"Come on, now, let's concentrate on the game. I've already forgotten what cards are safe," someone would say. Then we'd play furiously for five minutes.

Hope Hampton was the most spectacular. Her jewelry and clothes were incredible. Clear plastic purses that displayed the contents were then "in" and of course we all had them. Hope's bag always came in for the most ohh-ing and aah-ing. Everything in her bag was solid gold, with her name in diamonds on the top of each case or gadget.

None of us made any effort to compete with Hope when it came to jewelry. Mrs. Jerry Brady, who only joined us occasionally, came in one day proudly wearing a new diamond pin about three inches long. We all exclaimed over it, but Hope had a two-word crusher. "It's sweet," she said.

One day Hope got the farfetched notion that her ten-inch diamond brooch and bracelet were a little too ostentatious and decided to have them redesigned into smaller pieces. She put those and several other sensational items of jewelry in a paper bag and we marched down to Van Cleef and Arpels where Hope spent a couple of hours with the head designer thinking up new settings. When the session was finished, Hope said, "Say, Millie, why don't you have all your jewelry redesigned too?"

"OK," I said, taking off my wedding ring with its 13 diamond chips on top and extending it to the designer, "What can you do with that?"

Since my contact with Hope was almost entirely during those girlie luncheons and card games, I barely knew her husband Jules Brulatour. When he passed away, I didn't even think of going to his wake. I was at a gay cocktail party at the Waldorf all dressed up in sequins and feathers and looking slightly like a Babylonian whore when I was called to the phone. It was Hope.

"Listen," she said, "we're having the wake over at the Abbey and we're just about to say the Rosary. You're the only one I know who knows the words, so come on over here fast and bring some Catholics with you."

I hastily cased the cocktail party and singled out eight pals I was sure would know the Rosary. They didn't seem too anxious to go with me to the Abbey Funeral Home, but we made a deal. Bob and I promised to take them on to El Morocco afterward.

We piled into two taxis and told the drivers to wait while we went into the Abbey for a few minutes. When we reached the dimly-lit room the mourners were already on their knees reciting the Rosary. We slipped in quietly, dropped to our knees, and joined in. Many a startled glance was directed our way. The only teetotaler among my draftees was Joseph Timothy Patrick Sullivan, yet he was the only one who seemed moved. Tears were rolling down his cheeks.

When we got back into the taxis I said, "Joe, I didn't know you knew Jules so well."

"Jules who?" he asked.

A few months after Jules' death, Hope called and asked me if I thought it would be all right for her to start wearing her jewelry again.

"Jules gave it to you," I replied, "and I think he'd definitely want you to wear it to remember him by."

Several months after that Hope asked if I thought it would be proper for her to have dates.

"I'm sure Jules wouldn't want you to be alone and lonely, so why not?" I assured her.

About a month later Hope called again. "What am I going to do? All these fellows I go out with want to get too romantic."

"Well, what have you been doing so far when the going gets rough?" I asked.

"So far I've had pretty good luck by saying, 'remember, Jules' big brown eyes are looking at you out of heaven.'"

I guess that *would* be effective!

At night the Stork served as a co-ed meeting place. In the early forties it was far and away the most popular nightspot in New York, and had a protocol all its own. As Bob and I began to learn it, we felt we were really becoming New Yorkers.

I guess you might say we were squares on our first trip to the Stork after we moved from Washington. We were so uncertain about even being admitted that we asked George Preston Marshall to call and make a reservation for us. Once seated at a ringside table we became quite brave and cosmopolitan. Bob imperiously beckoned the headwaiter and asked, "What time does the floor show start?"

His "There is no floor show at the Stork Club," quickly made us hicks again.

The Bugs Baers and the Ed Sullivans were the ones who got us included in the so-called "in" group at the Stork. We soon discovered the astonishing fact that Billingsley did not present checks to newspapermen. That readily explained why there were so many columnists there every night, and why the Stork got so much free publicity. Efforts to pay a check at the Stork were rejected as if money had become useless. You can imagine what we felt like when the orchestra played "The Best Things in Life Are Free."

There was a night, though, when we happily thought we were going to be "on the cuff," but weren't. We'd gone to celebrate New Year's Eve with the Baers, Sullivans and Walter Shirleys. When we went we all fully expected to get a check because of the surcharge for the occasion, so we planned to order just one bottle of champagne and to keep the expense down as much as possible.

When bottle after bottle of champagne arrived at the table without our ordering them, we decided we were obviously to be treated after all. We relaxed, sang, blew horns and joined in the revelry with abandon. All except Walter Shirley. He had a bad case of laryngitis and could barely whisper. At 3 A.M., alas, Walter recovered his voice just long enough to say "Check, please" to a passing waiter. Wow! A check for over $300 was on our table.

I've never seen gaiety die so quickly. Confetti stopped in mid-air, horns fell to the table, Bugs Baer's Uncle Sam hat and white beard suddenly went askew. There was deathly silence while the men divvied up the bill.

It was at the Stork Club that Bob and I were introduced to the snobbery that prevails at most New York restaurants and night-clubs. In Washington we had never known that it was impor-tant for one's reputation to sit within a certain square footage of a room where the same food and drink was being served all over. All the food came out of the same kitchen; all the liquid out of the same bottles. It was enough in our early days just to *be* at the Iron Gate Inn, the Green Parrot or Child's. To have considered it vital where we sat in those places would have been as incom-prehensible to us as it would be for an astronaut to be told he was in a gauche orbit. The fact of orbiting would seem to him more important, as the fact of "eating out" did to us.

We soon learned that the Stork's snobbery began at the entrance. The first degree of acceptance was being escorted past the gold chain strung across the doorway. That was the hurdle Bob and I resented the most. It really hurt us to see eager young couples, as we'd so recently been, and lonely servicemen barred from entrance. A pint-size maitre d' named Gregory was high priest of the gold chain, and if he was in doubt about admitting someone he would glance toward Billingsley, sitting just inside, for a sign of clearance.

Billingsley was most adamant about not allowing Negroes into the Stork. One night George Jessel broke that barrier. He appeared at the door at an off hour, when the club was not yet filled, with Lena Horne on his arm. Despite the fact that Lena was a beautiful, well-dressed woman at the height of her success as a singer in New York, Gregory kept his hand on the chain to bar entrance.

"Have you a reservation?" he coldly demanded of Jessel, who was ordinarily a most welcome patron.

"Yes," said Jessel.

"Who made it?"

"Abraham Lincoln," Jessel retorted, as he brushed Gregory aside and walked on in with Lena.

The second degree of snobbery at the Stork, once inside the gold chain, was being escorted into the inner sanctum, the Cub Room. To be really "in," seemingly, you had to be seated near the front of that room. If you were seated at or very near the big round table in the corner, called Table Fifty, you had it made. Then you were sure to receive a big bottle of Sortilège or LeGalion perfume and a pair of red suspenders, Billingsley's highest tribute to his favored customers.

Billingsley had a financial interest in the perfume, along with Morton Downey and Arthur Godfrey, and there were times when he made more money out of his perfume business that he did out of the Stork.

As we became acclimated to New York and its mores we learned that *where* one is seated is a federal case in all the top restaurants. There is a definitely designated section for favored customers almost everywhere. The most laughable example is at El Morocco. The section of the room beyond the dance floor is reserved for those the headwaiter considers "nobodies," and had come to be called "Siberia." They'll put up so many extra tables on the dance floor to accommodate favored patrons who refuse to sit in the half-empty "Siberia" that it's sometimes impossible to dance. The smug "in" group sometimes look enviously at the

out-of-towners who are thoroughly enjoying themselves in comfort on the wrong side of the room, not even realizing they're in
Siberia.

The same snobbery prevails at Club "21." There are customers who will go elsewhere to eat if there's no space for them
in the first room of the bar. Otherwise they'd be afraid of losing
face. Those are the people who *must* be near the front of the
main room at the Colony, in the little cramped section at the
right in Trader Vic's, in the small room just before the orchestra
at Luchow's, at one of the four front banquettes at Toots Shor's,
or along the drafty entrance corridor leading to the main room
at La Caravelle. I've often wondered if the owners of those
restaurants decree that the draftiest, least comfortable areas are
"in" in order to keep them filled. If so, it works!

The best period in the Cub Room at the Stork was the short-
lived one when customers were allowed to play gin rummy at the
tables. A tall, courtly headwaiter named Jack Spooner went
from table to table exchanging pleasantries. I remember his
"Spooner" sandwich. It's made with a delicious hot mixture
which I think is mainly diced chicken.

The Cub Room was more fun and games than any other New
York spot before or since. Everyone knew one another, and every
night was a party.

It was then that we started playing the category game that
later took me through long stretches on planes and buses. Somebody announces a category, and everybody within hearing tries
to think of names to fit it. Say the category is water. There's Ethel
Waters, Louise Brooks, Arthur Lake, Nelson Eddy, Dinah Shore,
Rex Beach, etc.

The trouble with this game is that you usually think of the best
names for a category when you're lying in bed. Sometimes you

wake up during the night and think of one. Then no matter what time of night it is you immediately pick up the phone and call whomever you were last playing the game with to relay your latest brainchild.

Rosemary (Mrs. Earl) Wilson, Houston columnist Maxine Mesinger and I carry those nocturnal phone calls to ridiculous extremes.

"Millie, this is Rosie. How about Hyman Goldberg for the body?"

"I'll do you one better — Peter O'Toole."

We'll both scream with laughter and hang up the phone.

Or it might be me calling Maxine.

"How do you like Charlie Fawcett for water?"

"Love it," Maxine will say, and hang up. Then she'll call back in a few minutes with "How are Sir Samuel Hoar, Sir Anthony Trollop and King Lear for sex?"

When I think of the surprised operators. . . . Oh well, that's what the Stork did to people.

Maybe even more hectic was the Stork Club's balloon night. The ceiling of the main room would be covered with floating balloons and at midnight they'd be released. All of the women in the place, from Siberia to the Cub Room, would scramble around madly to catch a balloon. Some of them had slips of paper inside indicating prizes, which ran the gamut from a poodle puppy to champagne to a free dinner for two at the Stork. Nothing was more bizarre than watching women wrapped in furs and diamonds fighting like tigresses to snare a balloon!

I'm sure one of the most unusual sights at the Stork Club occurred in the ladies' room during the period I was nursing Barry. Nursing a baby is extremely gratifying and I highly recommend it, but it *is* confining to have to be on tap, so to speak, every four hours. I was fairly content to stay at our summer place in Rye, but Bob suggested I get back into the swing of things. Dr. Damon finally came up with a solution. The nurse could give Barry a bottle for one nighttime feeding, and I could take along a breast pump to the Stork. My readers who have nursed babies know it's painful if you don't when it's time. I can understand why cows bellow at milking time.

At my milking time I'd stroll up to the ladies' room, get out my handy little gadget and get busy. I love to think of the amazed expressions I saw on the faces of the girls who came into the ladies' room.

The funniest nights at the Stork, and we still laugh about them, were TV nights. For a while, a TV show emanated nightly from a private room upstairs at the Stork, sponsored by Fatima cigarettes. The room was set up like the main room downstairs, and Sherman invited some of us to sit around the tables as background. We all accepted readily because it meant free drinks and dinner — and because we were hams and *wanted* to be on TV!

Sometimes we were asked to say a few words, but mostly the talking was done by Sherman and his special guests. Billingsley wasn't terribly quick and had a bad memory, so "idiot" cards with questions and answers were placed behind the guest he was interviewing. Questions were also pasted inside the rim of the coffee cup Sherman was drinking from so he wouldn't always be looking in one direction. We could barely restrain ourselves when we saw him turning his cup around and around straining to see the question pasted inside.

One night the guest was Princess Pacelli, niece of Pope Pius XII, and Sherman hadn't been filled in on her. When the conversation came to a standstill, Princess Pacelli grabbed at a straw. She noticed the Fatima cigarette ad on the table and said, "You know Fatima has great meaning for us Catholics. That's the name of a religious shrine in Portugal, except that we pronounce it FATima, rather than Fat-*ee*-ma as you do."

"Well, you're wrong," Billingsley said, concluding the interview.

Billingsley might have lasted indefinitely on TV if Toots Shor hadn't happened to be watching the show at home one night. Sherman's guest was Carl Brisson, and as he often did, Sherm was riffling through a batch of photographs and commenting on the various people depicted.

He spotted a picture of Toots Shor and for some reason said, "I wish I had the money he owes."

"Does he owe *you* any?" said Brisson.

"No, but he owes everybody."

Toots sued Billingsley for a million dollars for "defamation of credit," and collected $50,000, the biggest sum ever awarded up to that time without jury recommendation. This case is supposed to have set a precedent that slander on television is as culpable as slander in the printed word.

six

An Irish Shillelagh

◄§§► The shillelagh I found in the attic is one thing I'd never get rid of. It's what our little girl Debbie chose to bring home as a souvenir of her first trip back to Ireland — the land of her birth.

By the time Dennis was five years old it began to look as though my brief flash at fertility was over, and that we'd never have a little girl. We made overtures to several adoption agencies only to discover how difficult it is for a family that already had three children to adopt another one.

We'd assumed a happy family with a nice home would be an ideal place for a little girl. The adoption agencies didn't think that way.

"You already have a family," they'd say. "Why do you need another child? We have to take care first of these long lists of childless couples begging for babies."

"If there's such a demand for them why are there so many homeless babies?" we'd demand.

Then we'd hear the same speeches we heard before we

adopted Mike. "We have to be careful in our screening," they'd patiently explain. "We have to fit each baby into exactly the right home. We have to match the background of each baby to that of the adoptive parents and that means they should have the same religion, nationality and intelligence levels. This all takes time and the process is slow."

"Do you think a homeless baby gives a damn about the religion, nationality or even financial status of people who want to love him and give him a home?" Bob would demand angrily, as so many frustrated couples have demanded before and since.

In the end they reminded us that we were over thirty-five and shouldn't think of adopting a *baby* at all. They thought it would be impractical for a baby to have such old parents, and that we should think in terms of adopting an older child, say one ten or twelve.

"Here's a nice little boy now," we were told at one agency. "He's ten and has been in five different adopted homes. He's run away from all of them and been put under the charge of the juvenile court. Nobody can keep him in school and he has quite a personality problem by now, but maybe you could straighten him out."

I don't know why she thought so, since she didn't even think we could manage a baby. But she showed us a picture of a handsome little boy with the surliest, unhappiest face I've ever seen. Our hearts went out to him, but we had plenty of boys. We wanted a girl.

"Why don't you take a girl around 12 or 14, and she could help you around the house?" one mean-looking social worker suggested.

"We're looking for a little baby girl to love and cherish, not a domestic," were our parting words.

We'd almost given up when I saw a magazine piece by Dr. Robert Collis, an Irish doctor who had helped take care of the sick Jewish children of liberated Nazi concentration camps. In the end he had adopted the two most crippled children left over when the list was finally closed. At the time of the article, they were strong and healthy. I wrote Dr. Collis a fan letter, and by some divine inspiration, just before sealing the letter I opened it up again and added a postscript: "My motives are not noble like yours. I'd like to adopt a beautiful, perfect little Irish girl."

Dr. Collis wrote back immediately that he was in contact with three orphanages in Dublin and would look around for us. After much correspondence, he wrote he had found three ideal babies for us to choose from. Bob was in Israel on a story when I wired him the news. He stopped off in Dublin and took movies and still pictures of all three babies. When he got home he showed each of us the pictures separately. We all chose Debbie without a moment's hesitation. She was the one Bob had most wanted too, when he saw the children. She was not quite two, and had curly chestnut hair, violet eyes, and a dimple in her chin. In fact, she was the most beautiful baby I had ever seen.

We wired Dr. Collis and he set the wheels in motion, along with the help of the American Embassy. When it was arranged for Debbie to be flown over to us in care of a TWA steward, I sent Dr. Collis a pink velvet coat, leggings and hat for her to wear home.

As a woman who has given birth to babies and adopted them, let me tell you the joys of both events are really almost identical. When you take into your heart a child you want and need as she does you, instantly, on first sight, it's as if she *were* your own. From that moment, she *is* your own.

News that the "Considine baby" was arriving by TWA somehow reached Doug Edwards of CBS. He called Bob and said he'd like to send a camera crew to the airport and film the arrival as part of a television feature he was doing on adoption. Bob and I talked it over and decided we didn't want the baby to be a part of such a to-do in the first moments of her life in America.

"The poor darling will probably burst into tears when she sees us," I said, "and I don't want to have something like that televised."

So Bob called and explained. But the night before the arrival — the DC-4 was already in flight across the ocean — Doug called again and made such a good case we agreed.

The plane arrived ahead of time, so early in the morning we just barely made it to LaGuardia on time. In fact, as we drove toward the field the plane swept low over the runway on its landing approach, and all of us were filled with the most tense expectation.

The steps were being placed against the side of the plane as we arrived, a bit out of breath. The CBS cameras were there and I remember saying a little prayer that Debbie wouldn't cry when she was turned over to the outstretched arms of a family she had never seen. All three boys, of course, were part of the reception committee.

Then the door of the plane opened and TWA's chief steward came out with our baby in his arms, dressed in the pink outfit I'd sent over. Even though we had never seen each other, Debbie, I insist, recognized me. As the steward carried her down the steps, Debbie calmly looked over the two dozen people standing at the foot of the steps and held out her arms to me, giving me the most beautiful smile I had ever seen in my life. *I* burst into tears and ruined Doug's show!

We decided to take Debbie to California to be christened in the Church of the Good Shepherd, with Louella Parsons as godmother and hotelman Hernando Courtright as godfather. We figured she'd always be sure of a "plug" and a room whenever she visited Beverly Hills.

Debbie looked her most adorable the day of the christening, all dressed up in a fluffy white organdy dress. She did not act the way she looked though. She took an instant dislike to Louella and kept trying to punch her throughout the ceremony. Louella is quite adept at ducking, but the constant sparring was distracting. When the ceremony mercifully ended, we tried to explain away Debbie's actions to Louella by saying, "She plays with her brothers that way — they taught it to her and she thinks it's fun." I'm not sure Louella was convinced. She didn't seem anxious to ride in the same car with Debbie.

Years passed before Debbie again showed any fondness for fist-fights. I suspect her brothers' ideas of playing prompted her to bring the shillelagh home from Ireland. She was thirteen then, and we took her to see her homeland. I'll tell you, we were a little afraid she might be so enchanted she'd never want to come home. Ireland's worst feature was on our side — it rained every single day. We were relieved to hear our daughter say, even before the tour was over, "This is fun, but can't we go home and go to the beach with the boys?"

We tried to show Debbie all of Ireland from the Book of Kells at Trinity College to the good values in tweeds at Cassidy's on O'Connell Street, from the Blarney Stone to Ennis, where Bob's paternal ancestors lived, Kilkenny where Bob's grandmother was born, Limerick where apparently Bennett Cerf was born, the Lakes of Killarney, the way the Irish Sweepstakes operate, the old castles, the thatched roof cottages, the lovely, warm people. We'd been to Ireland often, but with Debbie we saw it with new eyes.

While around Dublin we stayed at the Old Conna Hill Hotel in County Wicklow, mainly because a friend of ours, Count Cyril McCormack, was manager. Cyril is a weatherbeaten, rugged and charming Irishman who happens to be a "Count" because his father, Irish tenor John McCormack, was made a Papal count. He loved entertaining his little compatriot Debbie. .

Once Cyril planned a picnic on the moors. If you're visiting Ireland, try not to plan many outdoor events! We could barely see through the drifting mists and intermittent rain, but did manage to meet many of the bundled-up, pink-faced men with hip boots digging peat on the bleak moors. Their shovels were shaped so as to bring out a perfect foot-long block of peat, which really looked like mud, with each spadeful. Then they stacked it in piles to dry. How it ever does in that weather I'll never know. It must, though, since it's the main source of fuel for the poor in Ireland. The only color on the gray-green hills was the bright yellow of gorse growing rampant. Even the sheep were gray-green except for the bright-colored brands on their sides.

We drove for what seemed like hours, getting colder by the minute. It's hard to find a place for a picnic in the rain. Cyril finally took us to an abandoned house by a lake. Once we'd started a fire in the fireplace it was a great place for picnicking.

Since Ireland's biggest business is the Sweepstakes, we spent an afternoon at the Irish Hospital Sweepstakes building in Ballsbridge. There's a great single room that covers four acres and is an eighth of a mile long from front to back. That's where the 3,000 clerical workers stay. They're mostly women and earn about $1300 a year. Six atlases are used, and a large board at the side of the room indicates tickets are sold in 190 countries. I never even realized there were 190 countries! But there are Irish people in such places as the Cameroons, Nyasaland, Seychelles, Togoland and Littonia, who make the tickets available to the natives.

Three drawings are held a year, the intake varying from time to time. Twenty-five percent of the money is set aside for hospitals. The amount of money that comes in determines the number of tickets drawn.

The room set aside for the drawings is dominated by a mammoth gold-colored drum which is nine feet in diameter, twenty-two feet long, and weighs seven tons. The drum contains 48 small openings for drawings, but only one round opening at the end through which the man who cleans and paints the interior of the drum can enter. One day, Gracie Fields crawled in to investigate. The painter, not realizing anybody was inside with him, started the drum whirling around. It was a screaming, disheveled, and no longer curious Gracie who finally emerged.

Before the counterfoils are put into the big drum, they are first put into two special machines where they are blown and mixed up by compressed air for three days. No one can complain the tickets aren't well mixed.

Six nurses at a time do the actual drawing from the gold drum under the watchful eyes of the police and dignitaries filling the room. Each nurse must hold up her hand and spread her fingers before reaching into the small aperture to draw, and she can't possibly see inside because of a rubber suction apparatus just inside the aperture that encases her hand. After the drawing is finished, the remaining counterfoils are left in the drum until just before the next drawing, at which time the drum is cleaned out and painted.

The names of the horses are drawn from a separate glass drum. This drawing room has large murals of racing scenes around two sides, and across another side of the room are large oil paintings of eight all-time great jockeys — Steve Donoghue, W. R. Johnstone, Joe Canty, Mornington Wing, Gordon Richards, Martin Molony, E. C. Elliott and Fred Archer.

Naturally we were all inspired to rush out and buy all the Sweeps tickets we could find. And, surprisingly, that's not easy. We bought ours mostly from bellhops and in cigar stores. Debbie spent several months deciding what to buy with her winnings — and, of course, learned what a cruel world this is.

From Dublin we drove to Cork, then up through the emerald West along the gently curving roads that had been there centuries before anybody ever thought of an automobile. We'd stop sometimes just to sit and look at ivy-clad ruins of castles. You can hear the laughter of better days — and the screams after Cromwell's pillage. At least according to Bob, Cromwell was always the heavy. Bob was working on *It's the Irish* at the time.

"You Irish have long since buried the hatchet with the British," he'd tell Debbie, "but not with Cromwell. He's been hated here for three hundred years. When the people of the little town of Drogheda resisted his army, you know what he did? When he finally captured the town, he killed everyone — women, children, priests, nuns. And you know what he did then? He sat down and praised God. Gave God credit for inspiring him to kill all those Irish Catholics!"

Or sometimes Bob would tease her about Ireland:

"You know what George Bernard Shaw wrote about Ireland? I've got it here somewhere. He was living in London at the time and made a short trip to Ireland — like we're making — and when he went back to London he wrote:

> At last I went to Ireland
> 'Twas raining cats and dogs;
> I found no music in the glens,
> Nor purple in the bogs.
> And as for angels' laughter in
> The smelly Liffey's tide —
> Well, my Irish daddy said it,
> But the dear old humbug lied.

But mostly Bob would fill Debbie with just cause to be proud of her heritage. He'd tell her stories about how the Irish fought in George Washington's army to help give America the freedom they couldn't have. And stories of the Great Potato Famine, and the emigrations to America, and how badly the Irish were treated when they first arrived there — and how hard they worked to change that.

He'd tell her about his own experiences in Ireland too:

"On my first trip to Ireland, I was in line at the immigration desk at Foynes with the rest of the people who got off the plane. When it came time for me to show my passport to the old Irishman behind the desk he squinted at the name, looked up at me and said, 'I was in jail with many a Considine.'

"Everyone laughed — just as you are both laughing now — but the old man wasn't laughing. He cleared his throat and in a loud voice said, 'It was an honor to be in jail during the Trouble.' And it was, of course. *Not* to have a jail record around the time of the Easter Rebellion in 1916 meant that you didn't care very much about helping Ireland fight for independence."

Bob had the last laugh on me, though, when I tried to kiss the Blarney Stone. It's very hard to do. It's even hard to get up to the stone on the narrow, worn steps of the old castle. It was built in 1446, and in places the steps are nearly worn away. Some five hundred years of use does tend to do that. No one ever thought of a handrail.

The stone is below the battlements on the southern wall about four stories high. To kiss it, you have to lie down flat on your back, lean your head down about a foot, upside down and backwards, then stretch out and try to reach the stone with your lips. A man holds your legs so you won't fall off.

Kissing the stone is supposed to confer eloquence, but I proved to be quite eloquent while trying to get to where I *could* kiss the damn thing. I never did. I got so dizzy I thought I was going to faint and had to be hauled up. Then my devoted husband and daughter showed me how easy it was for them.

I was more at home in Ennis. For one thing it seemed *ours*. Practically every shop on the curving, narrow main street had a sign "Considine's Bar," "Considine's Meat Market," etc. Even in the little graveyard every other tombstone had Considine carved on it!

We stayed at the Old Ground Hotel, which like the Dublin hotels, is nothing physically. Yet all of them seem charming because of the people in them — from the old ladies sitting around having tea, to the tiny bellboys and elevator boys (they're supposed to be fourteen before they start working but most of them must fudge a little) to the ruddy-faced, knickered travelers. That wonderful Irish coffee laced with Irish whiskey and topped with thick cream helps too.

I began to feel that the whole world was friendly and warm, so I decided we should call John Huston. Before we left home at least a dozen friends said, "If you ever get near Galway be sure to call John Huston. He's absolutely charming and you'll love each other." The map on the desk in our room indicated we weren't too far from Galway.

Some of those mutual friends had insisted John would invite us over to stay with him for a few days if he knew we were there. All through the trip I'd had that thought at the back of my mind. I thought it would be a nice clincher for the trip, to visit an American who preferred to live in Ireland.

We'd known John's wife Ricki Soma when she was a little girl and used to toe-dance around her father's restaurant, Tony's, on 52nd Street. In fact, Ricki and her mother were my first callers at the hospital when I had Barry. I thought it would be fun to see her again, and, of course, to meet the irresistible John.

"Before we make any dinner plans, let's give John Huston a call," I said to Bob. "We're only a couple of hours from where he lives."

Bob wasn't at all enthusiastic. "Who likes to get calls from friends of friends? He probably never heard of us."

"But we promised all those people we'd call him."

To shut me up Bob called.

"This is Bob Considine," he said, glaring at me over the phone.

"Yeah?" said Huston.

"We're in Ennis and several of our mutual friends (he named them) asked me to call you and say hello."

"Yeah? Well thanks," said Huston.

I could see from Bob's face things weren't going well, so I grabbed the phone.

"We've known your wife since she was a little girl," I enthused.

"Yeah? Well, she's not here now, she's in Paris."

"How is she?" Even I was beginning to waver.

"I guess she's okay, but as I said she's not here."

By now I gave up the idea of a weekend stay, but still had hopes for dinner.

"We thought perhaps we could get together for a drink or something," I trailed off weakly.

"Well I've got a dinner date and I'm just running out now," he said with finality. I barely had time to say good-bye.

It's lucky that like Louella, I'm a good ducker. Bob flounced off to a pub. Debbie and I had dinner alone in our room.

My favorite memory of that trip to Ireland is a ride we had around the Lakes of Killarney in a jaunting cart. Our toothless old driver told us Grace Kelly and Prince Rainier had ridden in the same cart just a few weeks previously and Grace had proudly told him a 21-gun salute was fired when her son was born.

"I wasn't all that interested," the old man confided to us, "so I said to her, 'that's nothing, when our Bishop's house-keeper had a baby they fired a Canon.' "

seven

An Antique Handkerchief

≈§§≈ The antique handkerchief I found in a trunk reminds me of someone who *was* vitally interested in everything said by Grace Kelly or anybody else connected with the movies — Louella Parsons, the dean of Hollywood columnists. I was with Louella when she bought a similar handkerchief for Rita Hayworth to carry when she married Aly Khan. We were in Paris at the time, and as accustomed as I am to short notice, that trip with Louella was about the shortest notice I ever had.

Louella was in New York en route to cover Rita and Aly's wedding in the South of France, and asked me to lunch during her brief layover. During lunch she said, "Why don't you come to Paris with me? I'll call and see if there's an extra seat on the plane." There was, and I went.

Bob was in Berlin at the time covering the end of the Berlin Airlift, and the trip sounded like an inspirational idea. I rushed home and double-checked my passport and clothes, then wired Bob "When you're finished there meet me in Paris at the George V Hotel." We took off that evening.

John Haskell, the husband of Louella's assistant (now successor) Dorothy Manners, and tiny Johnny Hyde, who was Rita's agent, were with us. Johnny was also Marilyn Monroe's first mentor and agent, and she was more or less faithful to him until he died of a heart attack not long after our Paris trip.

Traveling with Louella was like being in a royal entourage. Red carpets everywhere! Louella's suite was overflowing with flowers from movie companies and stars when we arrived, and the phone never stopped ringing. Everybody in Paris who was remotely connected with movies came to pledge Louella their undying devotion in person also.

A tearful Merle Oberon came by to give Louella all the details of how she had recently seen her fiancé killed in a plane accident. Nobody ever held anything back from Louella. They didn't dare, if they wanted to stay in her good graces. Louella wielded such power through her movie column it was really terribly important for movie people *to* stay in her good graces.

We went to endless parties at which Louella looked slightly vague as various people talked to her, and since she took no notes and didn't even seem to be listening, I was afraid she was missing a lot of good items for her column. But when we'd get back to her suite and I'd unzipped, unbuttoned, unsnapped and unhooked all her various layers of clothing before going to my own suite, she'd sit down and start writing laboriously in longhand. Next morning she'd show me the dozens of pages she'd written. The things she remembered! That vague, uninterested look was *some* gimmick. To get her attention, people would tell her much more than they'd meant to.

Louella had a great sense of humor, and it almost got us all into trouble one night. Errol Flynn took us to one of those Lesbian cellar joints on the Left Bank, and after we'd ordered drinks

and watched the girls dancing together for a while, Louella suddenly got up and cut in on one of the dancing couples. Hell broke
loose. All the girls converged on Louella and one of the dancers
she was trying to cut in on, the one with the short hair and man-
nish suit, pulled a knife. The manager of the place, Errol and
the two Johnnys made a flying wedge and extricated Louella,
then we were rushed through the kitchen, up the back cellar
steps, and into a car.

One night the four of us went to a nightclub on Place Pigalle.
As we were walking down the street afterward, a furtive-looking
character accosted us with, "You want to see exhibeeshon?" and
outlined the various types offered, including "a lady and a tiger,"
with the price list for each offering. It ran from $100 for the
lady and the tiger to $35 for more pedestrian attractions. Louella
and I wanted out. Fast. But the two boys were determined. They
pointed out that "an exhibition" is a definite part of tourism in
Paris, that we should see all sides of life, that everybody we know
has seen one at some time or another, that we shouldn't be prud-
ish spoilsports, etc. They convinced us.

Then they counted their money and discovered they only had
$50 between them, which meant we had to take the $35 job in
order to have enough money left over to have a Calvados and
get back to the hotel.

Our guide led us to a place around the corner called the Senate
Hotel and up three flights of rickety stairs to a little room that
contained a double bed, a washstand, a red rug, red wallpaper,
four straight chairs for us to sit on, and two bright, unclouded
light bulbs. The guide took the $35 and then went off in search of
"talent." We made the boys put their handkerchiefs around the
light bulbs to assuage our guilt.

During our fifteen-minute wait I noticed John Haskell's cigarette had fallen off the ashtray and was smouldering on the rug. "I can see the headlines now," I whispered to Louella, "Louella Parsons and wife of prominent Catholic layman perish in Paris bordello fire."

Louella wasn't listening. She kept moaning, "Where can I find a priest who can't speak English?"

Finally the door opened and in walked two unattractive gold-toothed women about thirtyish, and a handsome young man about twenty. Without a word they started to disrobe. That did it. Louella and I chickened out and bounded down the stairs, followed a minute later by the frustrated boys. We ran into the bar next door, and as we were downing our drinks and trying to find something innocuous to talk about, who should walk in but the "talent." They seemed to need a drink as badly as we did. The boys graciously invited them to join us, but Louella announced she had to get back to the hotel and file a column.

"Why don't you sleep in my suite with me tonight?" Louella suggested after we'd told the boys good-night in the lobby. It seemed like a good idea. Though it wasn't mentioned, I imagine both Louella and I had a vague idea even *we* might look good to the boys that night. It was a pretty farfetched notion of course.

Louella sat up in bed half the night writing out a column in longhand, which you can be sure did not include what Catholics call "an occasion of sin."

The next night while Louella was having dinner with a movie producer, the two Johns went off on their own (and I have a darn good idea where they went). I went out with an old friend, Roger Dann, a Frenchman who spent some time in New York as a singer and actor, to see "his" Paris. We visited several little offbeat bistros and ended up in a picturesque little place where Roger used to go as a young man.

Two accordion players were holding forth on a small balcony, and young French couples were doing a bouncy little dance with their arms wrapped about each other.

Suddenly someone stuck his head in the door and shouted, "Ils viennent." The mood changed instantly. Everybody sat down and started necking violently or looking ferocious. Out of nowhere appeared a fattish woman in a tight black satin dress, with a spit curl on her forehead and a rose behind her ear, accompanied by a bully in tight pants and striped jersey shirt. Then in through the door trooped a group of American tourists from a bus parked outside marked "Paris by Night." Satin dress and striped shirt went into a frenzied Apache dance during which two of the young men who had been dancing before pretended they were fighting over a girl and others pretended they were staggering to the bar or yelled obscenities.

The weird tableau lasted about ten minutes. Then the tourists marched back out to their bus, casting frightened glances behind them. Instantly, satin dress and striped shirt disappeared, the bouncy accordion music started again, and everybody was up dancing, laughing and singing. Roger told me the dancers were regular habitués who got drinks at a reduced rate for taking part in the nightly farce.

Bob arrived from Berlin the next morning, and Louella asked us all to go shopping with her to help pick out a wedding present for Rita Hayworth. Kingsbury Smith of INS had given her 10,000 francs (about $28 at that time) for the purpose. Apparently the Hearst empire was on an economy wave.

"Why not just give her the money?" asked Bob.

"Or a toaster," I suggested.

"We'll start at Cartier's," Louella announced.

We started at Cartier's, but that didn't take long. Then we

tramped up and down Rue Rivoli and Rue St. Honore for hours, our suggestions for presents becoming more ridiculous all the time.

As luck would have it we met Maxime deBeix for lunch and he solved the gift problem. Maxime was an old white-haired French gentleman who represented *VARIETY* in Paris for years. Ever since I'd met him through Abel Green, he'd been solving problems for me in Paris. He'd see that my room was always full of spicy nasturtiums. I never see or whiff that flower anymore without thinking of Maxime and Paris.

He took us to a tiny hole-in-the-wall French linen shop where we found a lovely antique lace handkerchief that had belonged to some queen. It was priced at $100, but after much behind-the-counter whispering on Maxime's part as to who Louella was and who was to receive the gift, Louella got it for her allotted $28. Rita loved it.

Maxime slipped a tiny parcel into my purse as we were leaving the shop, and when I got back to the hotel and opened it, I found a beautiful antique lace handkerchief — even prettier than the one Louella got for Rita. It had the initials L.R. on it, and Maxime told me later it had belonged to Lillian Russell.

When Louella and the two Johnnys took off for the wedding, Bob and I decided to drive down to see the shrine of Lourdes. Our TWA pals in Paris loaned us a car. Our driver, named Constant, was charming. The only hitch was that he spoke no English and my French was confined to such useful phrases as "J'ai faim," and "Ou est l'hotel le plus grand?" The latter was to insure a relatively comfortable place, for Constant was always trying to save us money by stopping at the very worst ones. Anyway, such useful phrases do not make for stimulating conversation. If any crises arose not covered by my useful phrases, we went through a

series of charades. By the time we got home I was able to win
every game we played. Bob overcomes his language barrier by
talking much louder or emitting grunts while pointing at what
he's trying to discuss.

Constant found some of the most marvelous little roadside
restaurants for us to eat in. In fact, some of them had better
paté maison than we could get in Paris. We sometimes bought
bread, York ham, paté, fruit and wine and had picnics under the
trees along the way.

As we neared Toulouse I remembered, for some reason, that
in all my long-distance conversations with Anny and the kids
since I'd left home nobody had mentioned the cat. Just before I
left for Paris our Siamese came into one of her numerous heats,
but this one seemed to bother her more than usual. Even the
older kids took pity on her and said, "For heaven's sake, Mom,
why don't you have her bred and take her out of her misery?"
I called a pet store and asked if they had a male Siamese for
breeding. They said they had just the mate and suggested I bring
my cat over and leave her there a few days.

We had a batch of paper wedding bells left from our last
anniversary party, so the kids and I bundled the cat into a basket,
covered it with the wedding bells and a "good luck" sign, and I
took her off for her rendezvous. I had a bad feeling about it the
minute I saw her fiancé — he was the meanest-looking lout I ever
laid eyes on. However, the die was cast, and unwillingly — left
our little maiden to her fate. She seemed so anxious.

The closer we got to Toulouse the more concerned I became.
It seemed strange nobody had mentioned the cat's mating. By
then I was much more interested in that marriage than I was in
the one Louella went to cover.

The minute we got into the hotel I put in a long-distance call to Anny. When I asked her about the cat there was a long, ominous silence. Then Anny said, "I wanted to wait with the bad news until you got home. She died at the pet store." What a heel I felt like. If only I'd played my hunch.

"How did the kids take it?" I asked.

"The little ones cried, of course," replied Anny, "but Mike keeps saying, 'what a way to go.' "

Then weeping Dennis got on the phone and wailed, "Mommy, our kitty died of marriage."

Bob, listening in on the extension, said, "Many of us have, son."

eight

Quarts and Quarts of Holy Water

◆§◈ So what does one do with a dozen, half-evaporated bottles of holy water? Give them to a church, rub the water on my increasingly numerous aches and pains? Is there a statute of limitations on how long holy water stays holy?

Our visit to Lourdes, the source of all my holy water, actually was quite soul-shaking for me. None of my religious training had prepared me for unquestioning acceptance of miracles. Even my conversion to Catholicism didn't. It seemed enough, at the time, to purge myself of the bigotry I'd acquired about the Catholic Church as a small-town, middle-western Protestant, and to accept the general idea of the Catholic Church, and to understand and accept the basic differences between Catholicism and Protestantism.

When I was a child in Oklahoma, we used to stand near the little local Catholic Church every Sunday just to watch its handful of parishioners emerge after attending Mass. There was something mysterious and alien about them, and much gossip about their strange rites. There were even dark whisperings about a tunnel that ran from the church to where the Pope lived. And imagine talking in Latin!

That sort of background was a bit difficult to overcome. Although a devout Catholic himself, Bob never pressured me to convert to his religion. We were married in the rectory of St. Mary's Church, and I did sign a paper testifying I would bring up any offspring as Catholics.

After we were married I attended Mass every Sunday with Bob, only to be with him. I found I felt more peaceful and closer to God than ever before. Then I began to wish I could follow the ritual along with the others. I felt I was missing something when Bob took Communion. He seemed so happy afterward.

One day I phone Monsignor Michael Ready, a worldly and hip priest who was doing what amounts to public relations for the Propagation of the Faith in Washington. He had gone to Mexico, posed as a bum in order to investigate, as an outsider, the persecution of priests and nuns during the time the leftist element of the Mexican Government began closing down churches and expropriating church property as well as American investments in Mexico. I asked if he'd be willing to instruct me as I'd decided I wanted to become a Catholic. When he agreed, I knew he'd try to make me understand the differences between Catholicism and Protestantism, rather than say "there it is — take it or leave it." He explained rather than persuaded.

After the lessons, we'd have a cocktail together and talk about sports. I couldn't help thinking of how we always had to hide the liquor when our Presbyterian preacher called at our house in Oklahoma. At the same time I was studying my catechisms I was also taking horseback riding and golf lessons. Monsignor Ready joked that I'd probably wind up genuflecting to a horse.

I've always been glad I became a Catholic, especially after the children came along. There are a great many things a Catholic has to accept on faith, and Lourdes was my first confrontation with the conflict of the natural and the supernatural. The natural was odious. Even if I'd never been exposed to religion before, I think I still would have winced at such souvenirs as a glass bottle shaped like the Blessed Virgin and crowned by a cork, or a miniature pair of crutches.

But the supernatural aspects of Lourdes were different — the crutches hanging from the rough stone walls of the cave near the Virgin's peaceful statue and the bubbling spring, for example. Surely the Church would never have perpetrated such a flimsy fraud. They must be real, else the owners of them could not very well have made their way away from the Grotto. Nearby, too, was an office whose task it has been for many years to check carefully on all claims of cures, part-cures and immunities. It's staffed by both Catholics and non-Catholics.

It was something of a relief to me to find that my misgivings about whether the Virgin had actually appeared to fourteen-year-old Marie Bernarde Soubirous (Bernadette) eighteen times back in 1858 had been shared for a time by the girl's contemporaries. That's understandable, of course. I can imagine my own reaction if Debbie walked into the kitchen one day while I was trying to keep a soufflé inflated and said, "Guess what, Mom, I just had a nice long talk with Jesus's Mother."

Conditions around the place where Bernadette lived could not have been conducive to rapid-fire acceptance, either. The family was poor to an extreme, as the rickety "Maison Paternelle de Ste. Bernadette" testifies — in spite of the awful souvenir shoppe next door.

Thanks to that poor little girl, what might have been just another sleepy French village is now the mecca for the religious and sick from all over the world. Every resident in town knows the whole story by heart, and loves to tell it.

Bernadette's father François was a town loafer who had let an inherited and potentially-profitable mill go to seed. Her mother "had a sharp tongue, but she, too, was gregarious and unwisely openhanded." The mill was seized by creditors — hardly a fitting prelude to a Heavenly visitation — and the family was evicted. They had to move into a room in the town's abandoned two-room "cachot," once a dungeon-jail.

The sickly Bernadette was farmed out as a shepherdess for her health and to provide her with food. In her loneliness, she became a contemplative child with a mind of her own. She returned to the village in her early teens and lived with her family in their single room. To help out, she served as nursemaid to her younger brothers and sisters and foraged for firewood along the river Gave, which flows through Lourdes.

The Gave carried lots of kindling into a grotto in a cliff called Massabielle. Neither of the younger children with her was aware of what Bernadette was later to describe as a sudden great wind and the appearance, as if suspended from the grotto's wall, of a young girl in classic white robe, white veil and blue sash, softly reciting the Rosary. Terrified, Bernadette dropped to her knees, found her own Rosary, and began to speak its decades of Hail Marys. When the vision passed, she told the children she had seen a "beautiful lady."

Bernadette must have been a determined girl to withstand the doubt and ridicule that greeted her story at home and in the neighborhood. She returned to the grotto the following Sunday and once again described the vision. Two adult women accompanied her the third time, saw nothing, but marveled at her story. She had been given instructions by the Virgin to return for the next fifteen days straight. She said the Virgin had promised to reward her "not in this world, but the next." On her sixth visit the town's best-known doctor, a man named Dozous, went with her. He said he thought she was sane after an examination following her account of what she had just seen and heard. The town officials questioned her sharply. They apparently felt it was all a hoax which, when exposed, would bring discredit to the town. But she conducted herself with great dignity.

During her ninth visit, while she prayed, a spring of water broke through the porous rock at the point where her gaze was centered. It remains to this day the source of the waters of Lourdes.

After the sixteenth visit, Bernadette told the doubters — who were still in the majority — that the "beautiful lady" had said to her, "I am the Immaculate Conception."

In 1862 the Bishop of Tarbes, the top Church authority in the whole department of the Hautes-Pyrenees area, put his stamp of approval on the miracle. He decreed that "the apparition which called itself the Immaculate Conception, which Bernadette both saw and heard, is none other than the Most Holy Virgin."

Bernadette was thereafter hounded by the curious from miles around. They had no difficulty finding her, for the family remained in their one-room home. Finally, at the age of twenty-two, she left Lourdes to become a Sister of Charity and Christian Education nun, at the convent of St. Gilhard in Nevers. It was a hard life, and she had never fully recovered from her childhood troubles. She died when she was thirty-five. She was made a saint half a century later on December 8, the Feast of the Immaculate Conception.

Bernadette and her visions became very real as we walked

down the long esplanade leading to the basilica, the Church of the Rosary and the Grotto with its spring of healing water. The day we were there, a pilgrimage of sick and crippled people from Belgium was lined up all the way down the esplanade and around the basilica. You could feel in the air the despair mixed with hope and faith. We had to turn away from the sight of the people as they lay there on litters or sat in wheelchairs, each accompanied by a healthy relative or nurse. Some were horribly deformed, disfigured or shrunken with illness. All had the same look in their eyes as the priests went from one to another, praying and sprinkling them with holy water. We found ourselves praying as hard as we could for the miracle they were all fervently praying for — the miracle that had been achieved by previous visitors who had left their crutches and braces behind, now lining the walls of the Grotto.

The spring has been channeled into a pool inside the Church, and trembling invalids are sometimes led through the pool for its healing effect.

Along the side of the basilica is a long trough with spigots where people were filling bottles of holy water. Someone was selling quart-sized metal containers, so we bought a half dozen of them and filled them from the spigots (that part didn't seem very spiritual).

I left Lourdes believing to a greater extent than disbelieving. But that wasn't true of the Customs men. They seemed suspicious of quarts of holy water. One even tasted some.

A private audience with Pope Pius XII did even more to strengthen my bond with the Catholic Church than the visit to Lourdes had done. If I had to choose the one person in the world I'm happiest to have met, I'd name gentle Pope Pius. I was overwhelmed.

The mode of dress for an audience with the Pope is quite circumscribed. Ladies must wear black dresses with high necks and long sleeves, and a black mantilla or veil over the hair. The men must wear dark suits.

As you're ushered in through the various phases of approaching His Holiness you become more and more impressed and nervous. First the Swiss Guards, in their colorful but slightly ridiculous uniforms designed by Michelangelo in a moment of pique, escort you through the gates and to the door. Then you're taken over by several elevating orders of Church officials, waiting successively in room after room. Finally you wait in a large room where the Pope conducts group audiences, with a throne at one end.

We peeked in while he was holding a group audience and were amazed that the Pope was familiar with the language of each one of the group, as he paused to speak to them individually for a moment.

After that group left, we sat in that enormous room where the group audience was held and waited while the Pope retired to his study.

"What on earth shall I say to him?" I asked Bob.

"Don't worry, he'll carry the ball," Bob assured me.

Bob didn't know me. I'm afraid in my nervousness I gave my standard first greeting: "I'm glad to meet you, I've heard so much about you."

nine

Home Movies

୫§§୬ Naturally, we couldn't take any movies — or pictures of any kind — during our audience with the Pope. But for almost every other occasion we have reels of film to refresh our memories. Daguerre, with his camera that led to the invention of movies, did a lot more toward stimulating total recall than the discoverer of sodium pentothal ever did!

We've always tried to keep our home movies from being the stereotyped portrayals of family and friends walking toward the camera, waving. True, like all doting parents, we've taken the usual thousands of feet of the kiddies from the day they each arrived. We've faithfully recorded each birthday or Hallowe'en party, each Christmas morning, camp life, picnics, all the club shows the kids have taken part in, the kids racing their boats through Deal Lake, flying above Niagara Falls in a helicopter, water skiing in Monte Carlo, surfing in Hawaii, etc. Everything from Mike's first tricycle to Debbie riding a camel in Tangiers. If any kid of mine ever gets on a psychiatrist's couch and starts talking about his lousy childhood, I'll just whip out some movies!

The best thing about movies is never losing any of your past (I guess that can be bad too). The children will never have to strain to recall a certain pal or incident. I remember how impossible it was to walk through our living room in Allenhurst at night. The floor was always full of neighborhood kids drinking cokes and watching the home movies. Occasionally we'd hear a yelp of delight as someone would recognize himself at a much younger age.

Our house-guests were never freeloaders. The fee at our house was having to watch some of our travelogues. Bob took some interesting movies of his trips with President Eisenhower to Korea and the Far East, with Vice President Nixon to Russia, and through the United States with Khrushchev. But they're only interesting if you like airplanes. Bob loves them. If a plane comes within miles of where he's taking a movie, he'll immediately leave the subject and zoom up to the plane.

I lost what, to me, would have been a priceless shot of me being kissed simultaneously by John Wayne and Kirk Douglas on a movie set in Hawaii once. Just as they leaned toward me to kiss me for my own movie, a plane took off near Pearl Harbor. Bob immediately zoomed the camera up toward the plane and missed the shot of us.

I always thought I took better movies than Bob did anyway, and the only time I relinquished the camera to him was for shots of me. That's why all of our movies show me at my worst — looking bossy and mouthing instructions to Bob.

But since I always splice our home movies myself, I do have a certain advantage. I could cut out my own bad parts, and sometimes change the actions around to suit my own purposes. I did a particularly marvelous job of splicing the water skiing movies taken in Acapulco.

I'd gone down to visit Sloan and Bill O'Dwyer, then our Ambassador to Mexico, and one day Sloan, who is an excellent water-skier, tried to teach June Smith and me how to water-ski. I was most inept. I simply could not stand up on the skis, and was pulled through the water for miles in a squatting position, getting the most colossal douche in history. Bill took movies of the whole sequences for me, and later on I was able to splice them in such a manner that I was seen starting off, and the next shot was of June skiing beautifully off in the distance. We're pretty much the same size and build, so. . . .

One night when all the neighborhood kids were looking at our movies I heard them howling with raucous laughter. They sounded just like I would have if, as a kid, I found one of my "adults only" movies. Sure enough, in full view was the one I took of Nancy Holmes undressing. Nancy and I had flown in a little charter plane from Honolulu to Maui, and when we saw a deserted beach that looked inviting, we decided to land and have a swim. Naturally there was no bath-house in which to change into our bathing suits, so we had to do it on the beach, out in the open. I had my movie camera with me and kept it trained on Nancy during the whole business of her wriggling out of her slacks, shirt and girdle and wriggling into a bathing suit. She yelled invectives at me the whole time but there was nothing much she could do about it. Her frantic efforts to hide her more interesting parts while changing made a hilarious movie reel. Even the neighborhood kids thought so!

Sometimes we'd have to sit through a whole 400-foot reel of travelogue just to see one funny shot we wanted to look at. We saw the reel on Italy so often we got to know all the landmarks by heart, just so we could laugh at the kissing interlude between me and Art Buchwald in Rome, which only consumed

ten feet of the reel. The kissing bit happened quite innocently
and unexpectedly.

Art and I were sitting in the bar of the Excelsior Hotel passing the time of day with some pals, when one of Art's friends
stopped by the table. "Well, you'll never guess what happened to
me," he said. "I just got arrested for kissing my girl good-by at
the railroad station." He insisted there is a Roman law that nobody can kiss in public. In Rome, that's hard to believe. Buchwald
and I decided to see for ourselves. We thought it would make a
funny column for both of us if we got arrested kissing in public.
I handed my movie camera to one of our pals to record the
scene.

Art and I walked out to the corner on Via Veneto and waited
until we saw two policemen standing across the street. When we
were sure they were looking our way, Art and I gave each other
a pedestrian little kiss. No response. Then we walked over and
stood right in front of the cops. We made it much better this
time. "Pazzas Americanis," they said and walked away. . . .
No column, but a bad cigar taste in my mouth plus a funny
movie shot.

I always got a private snicker out of watching the movies I
took in Florence. There was one unshootable incident. I was
having dinner with San Francisco columnist Herb Caen and his
wife at a hill-top restaurant overlooking the whole city. We sat
there, almost in a trance, looking at the lights of the city below
and listening to the soft Italian music.

We were all dying to dance but couldn't because there were
two girls and only one man. While I was trying to talk the Caens
into dancing and lying that I didn't mind sitting alone, a very
handsome man in a dinner jacket leaned over and said,

"Wouldn't you like to dance?" At that moment even an offer from a strange man seemed like an answer to a maiden's prayer. I jumped up and said, "Oh yes, I'd love to!"

"Oh, I'm sorry," he murmured, "I'm the headwaiter. I was only suggesting some of you take advantage of this nice music."

I've always thought if he had any class he would have danced with me anyhow, even if it meant his job.

That wasn't the first time I goofed with identity and it probably won't be the last. The very worst was the time in Paris when Prince Aly Khan invited me to attend the Grand Prix with him and Bettina, and said he'd send someone to pick me up. I didn't quite catch the name of the young man who came to fetch me. When he suggested I sit in the front seat with him, I said I thought I'd be more comfortable in the back. I thought he was some sort of chauffeur and that it wouldn't look right for me to drive up to the track sitting next to him in the front seat.

Aly was waiting for us when we arrived at the track. I felt like kicking myself when Aly said, "I guess you've already met my son Karim, haven't you?" It was the new Aga Khan I'd spurned.

There's one reel I have from the summer Bob, Debbie and I went to Hawaii with Red Skelton, his wife Georgia and their daughter Valentina, that always brings back our whole warm friendship. I first met the Skeltons when I was doing a radio interview show for NBC Monitor and taped an interview with Red and his dying son Richard. Red was in New York en route back to California after taking Richard on a European tour to see, for the first and last time, all the churches, museums and landmarks that Red had hoped to show him little by little as he grew up. Richard had leukemia, but Red managed to keep the family atmosphere healthy and lighthearted for him.

The loss of Richard, and Red's own close calls with death have had a sobering effect on the family, but Red's audiences would never know it. Red is always the comedian when in public.

When Bob and I spent those two weeks in Hawaii with him, we marveled at his patience. Every single time a meal was served to us, someone would walk over to our table and ask Red to pose for a picture. Others would see the picture being taken and ask Red to pose with them too. We'd all be finished eating before he came back to the table and his meal would always be cold.

"It's when they stop asking that I'll worry," he'd say.

Whenever we all went shopping, if Red bought a Hawaiian shirt for himself and dresses for Georgia and Valentina, he'd also buy a shirt for Bob and dresses for Debbie and me. One day we went on the wildest shopping spree I've every seen. We went into a shop in Lahaina, Maui, and while we were browsing around we noticed there were no other customers in the store.

"It doesn't look like business is too good," Red said to the worried-looking lady in charge.

"No, it isn't," she replied, "in fact it's so bad we may have to go out of business."

That was all Red needed.

"Well, you've got a lot of nice stuff here," Red said. His eye fell on several bronze Buddhas in a corner. "You know I design Japanese gardens, and I've been looking for some Buddhas just like those. I'll take all of them."

Turning to the rest of us Red said, "Why don't we do all our shopping right here. It will save walking around. Pick out anything you want."

Georgia and I concentrated on the jewelry counter, while the girls dived into the racks of clothes and bathing suits. I idly examined an Indian necklace of enamel and rubies then turned to look at something else. Red thrust the necklace into my hands and said, "It's yours, I just bought it for you." Georgia found a star sapphire she admired and it was instantly hers. Two hours and $10,000 later we walked out, leaving behind the happiest store owner in Hawaii.

As we walked on down the street a crowd, as usual, started following Red. He was performing all kinds of antics for the fans' grinding cameras, so we put our movie camera to work too.

When we passed the "Old Whalers" bar Red said "Wait a minute" to his fans and ducked inside. A minute later he came out the swinging door stumbling around in his best drunk act. They loved him. When we passed a pawn shop Bob said to Red, "Go in and take off your shirt as if you'd lost your shirt in the hock shop."

Red went him one better. I was peeking through the window of the shop from the side and saw the girl clerk inside look more and more horrified as the strange man walked in and took off not only his shirt, but also his suit, shoes and socks and walked out in his underwear. It made a hilarious shot, especially when Georgia grabbed him by the ear and marched him back in to put on his clothes.

One day on Waikiki Beach we all took a catamaran ride, along with Toots Shor, who had just arrived in Honolulu. During the ride Toots drank a whole pint of brandy he'd brought and was ready for anything. Word had spread along the beach that Red was coming in and a mob was assembled to see us land.

"Look at all my fans there waiting for me," Toots roared. He stood up on a bench, weaving from side to side and yelling to "his" fans. He gave them an even bigger laugh than Red did with his mugging when a big wave hit the catamaran and Toots toppled to the deck.

We couldn't help noticing that Red whipped out a notebook and took notes constantly throughout the day and evening. Red told us he's taken voluminous notes on everything that happened and practically everything said since he was ten years old. Every so often he has all the notes transcribed and bound in books. He'll certainly never have any trouble writing his autobiography! He'll have ready-made illustrations too. He must have fifty cameras, and carries three or four of them around with him, snapping pictures continuously. And the pictures are easily as good as professionally-taken ones.

When we later visited the Skeltons at their Palm Springs home we discovered Red paints pictures as well as he takes them. The walls of his home are lined with his terrific paintings. Predictably, his subjects are usually clowns.

I've never seen anyone enjoy being at home as much as Red does. The Skeltons spend every possible moment in Palm Springs, where their home adjoins the Tamarisk golf course. "Why should I go away from home," he says, "when eventually everybody comes to me. Everybody that plays golf anyhow." It's true. As the Skeltons sit around their pool, all the golfers eventually get to the nearby hole. In just one afternoon while I was sitting with the Skeltons, the golfers who stopped by to chat a minute included Frank Sinatra, Bing Crosby, Groucho Marx and Governor Pat Brown.

When he isn't painting or lounging around the pool, Red is busy working on his Japanese garden or reading in the Japanese tea-house he built himself. He's such an expert on planning and executing Japanese gardens he's done them for several friends and even for a couple of hotels.

It's such a pleasant experience to re-visit all the places we've been, re-live the fun, and become re-acquainted with all the old friends seen in our home movies, that I decided we'd simply have to find room in the apartment for the whole lot. After all, there *are* quiet evenings even in the city . . . times when one likes to relax and stroll back through Memory Lane.

ten

Autographed Photo of Gamal Nasser

উত্তর Ada is a fine old name, especially on my mother. It's fine too on the little town in Oklahoma. But on me, it had to go. Mildred didn't do either. I've never yet read a book about a trollop who wasn't called Mildred, from *Of Human Bondage* on. Millie, though, suits me great, so that's what I became — except on my first passport. It said, "Give your full name," and like a dope, there it was, big and bold. "Ada Mildred Anderson Considine." So now I have to hide my beautiful autographed picture of Nasser — autographed "To Ada, with the best wishes of Gamal Nasser" — with that dumb old passport.

I got the picture on our first trip to Egypt in 1955, shortly before Nasser was elected the first President of the Republic. I remember when some of the columnists on the TWA junket we were on were discussing the forthcoming election with him. I think it was George Dixon or Hal Boyle who asked, innocently, whether women would be voting. Nasser didn't make many friends among the girls with his vehement reply:

"Of course not. Women belong in the fields or in the kitchen."

But he made plenty of friends because of his looks. What a big, virile sexy-looking fellow he is. And quite charming too. He was also pretty smooth politically. He and his family were still living in the barracks, even though he was Premier.

I was flattered when he drew me aside as we were leaving and asked if I'd like an autographed picture. "I'll have it sent to your hotel," he said, flashing his fierce black and white smile. He must have called the desk clerk to get my first name from my passport. My terrible secret was no longer between me and the Immigration officers.

That's when I began a major "drop Ada" campaign with the passport people. A few years ago, I won. In fact, it was a double victory. I also got them to lop Coyle off as my birthplace. Oklahoma alone is sufficiently confusing to the Immigration people abroad.

I've only met one person in the whole world who ever heard of Coyle, Oklahoma. (That's understandable. My advent there swelled the population to 201.) One night somebody brought a Dr. Boysell to a candlelight Christmas party we had in New York. Like most women, whenever I hear the word "doctor" I think of my random ailments. I inflicted on that poor man what doctors all over the world must dread at parties. I maneuvered him into a corner and got into a detailed account of my anatomical malfunctions, labor pains and various other intimate details. Dr. Boysell, to my surprise, was fascinated. That spurred me on. I traced back to all of my childhood illnesses for that nice doctor, and finally got to my birth in happy old Coyle, Oklahoma. Dr. Boysell said, "Why that's the most amazing coincidence I've ever heard of. That's where I preached my first sermon." Then I turned green for the doctor. The same shade I turned when I saw "To Ada" on Nasser's picture.

The whole trip to Egypt wasn't a dud like that photo, though. We were thrilled from the first, as we flew in low over the Pyramids and Sphinx and saw the sharp dividing line between green vegetation and an endless stretch of desert.

Dr. Malik had just uncovered a solar boat that some ancient Pharaoh had ordered buried near him so he could use it in spirit-form for his ascension to heaven to join the sun-god Re (and maybe for a trip through the River Styx). We were taken through the excavations and walked over the shaky planks in semi-darkness.

Mena House, where we stayed, is fairly close to the Pyramids, and there are camels parked across the street for short trips. One time, we saw a magnificent sunset with the Sphinx silhouetted against it. George and Ymelda Dixon and Bob and I just sat spellbound on our camels. For once we were all speechless.

Egypt has variety, though, and most nights we hopped from one nightclub to another to watch the belly-dancers. (In those days the dancers' bellies were exposed and we could easily follow their unbelievable convolutions. Some fink came along later and insisted the girls wear at least gauze coverings.) The men went wild over the girls. But the belly-dancers made it quite plain they preferred girls. Especially big, busty blonde girls!

Once at a tent party in the Sahara, at least twelve of them, one by one, tried for my lap. I kneeled down on my knees so I had no lap for them to sit on, but one dewy-eyed plump dancer — I guess out of lap frustration — took me by the hand and said, "Come outside with me and I'll teach you how." I assume she meant "how to dance the belly-dance," but Bob suddenly decided it was time to leave.

In spite of the abrupt ending, that tent party was like a page from the Arabian Nights. We all gathered at the Cheops Pyramid at sunset. You haven't really seen a sunset until you've seen one on the Sahara, when the desert and sky merge. Sitting at the foot of Cheops was a group of Egyptian musicians in robes and tarbushes playing plaintive Oriental music on reed and string instruments. There were four or five magnificent-looking Egyptians with dark skin and flashing white teeth prancing about on fine white Arabian horses. They all looked exactly like Omar Shariff.

For transportation, there were camels with silk howdahs on their backs, camels with colorful fringed coverings, donkeys and pony carts. It took us ages to decide which to use. By the time we were all mounted and the caravan started moving across the desert there was a full moon. The musicians continued playing as they walked along with us. The Arabian horses pranced and danced among us. It was unearthly, incredible, wild. . . .

Not even my dragoman could spoil it for me. Through all the exotica he kept yelling "okey-dokey," "roger-dodger," "you're keeling me," and "super-colossal Brooklyn" to show his appreciation of Americans. Too bad I wasn't feeling homesick.

By the time we reached the huge silken tent, spread like a mirage on the darkening desert, the moon was high and the silence was broken only by wafts of eerie flute music, and a few "super-colossal Brooklyns!" When we entered the tent we saw how rich shieks must have lived. Luscious, silky Persian rugs covered the sand and all about were huge tufted pillows, camel-stools, low brass tables and water-pipes. All around were lamps of vari-colored glass. At one end of the tent were charcoal braziers with dozens of whole lambs roasting on spits. A platoon of waiters in long white robes flowed about, serving drinks and those rich, oily Egyptian hors d'oeuvres.

The adventurous ones of our group pounced on the pillows

and started smoking the water-pipes. All of us found ourselves lolling about like Cleopatra — Elizabeth Taylor style. While we were drinking and eating there was continuous entertainment. First came a group of swishy mystics with long black beards and long white robes who did a ritual dance, bouncing around with such fervor that some of them frothed at the mouth and fell to the ground, exhausted. Next came a beautiful young man wearing almost nothing, whose act consisted mostly of leaping into the air and touching his toes with his fingers. The mystics loved him, applauding like mad from the sidelines.

Then there were the belly-dancers. Congressman Halleck and George Dixon got so carried away they loosened their shirt-tails, rolled up their trouser legs, and joined the belly-dancers in their own version of the dance. Somebody took a picture of Halleck and it made *TIME* Magazine. His Indiana constituents weren't amused.

The next day we were flown to Luxor where we took a felucca across the Nile to King Tutankhamen's tomb. Later we explored Karnak Temple, the monoliths and Queen Nefertiti's former abode and took pictures of all the sexy friezes. If you think our generation is immoral you should see what these old Egyptians used to freeze into their friezes!

On the plane back to Cairo we celebrated TWA vice-president John Collings' birthday. A huge birthday cake was unveiled, and we were all having so much fun roaming up and down the aisles drinking champagne the pilot decided to give us a longer ride and fly down over Port Said.

Laughter comes easily on free trips, and we were all having a ball. The only one asleep was George Dixon. Bob was standing beside George talking to Ymelda. Collings was hovering over his cake getting ready to cut it. Just then the pilot announced we were flying over Mount Sinai where Moses was given the Ten Commandments.

I made the mistake of saying "Wouldn't it be wonderful if Moses hadn't gone up that mountain? Think how much more fun we'd all have." My retribution for that irreligious remark was instantaneous. The minute the words were out of my mouth the plane hit the worst air pocket I've ever experienced. We all flew upward and landed in heaps. Sleeping George went straight up in a sitting position, and as he descended, Bob's glass of champagne spilled all over him. Collings had the softest and most comfortable landing of all of us. He landed in his cake!

Four years later it was junket-to-Egypt time again. This trip was for the opening of the Nile Hilton in Cairo. The 58 invitees included movie stars and singers as well as press and hotel people. But when the plane landed, the only one who got a cheer was Miiko Taka — "Sayonara" was currently playing in Cairo. However, the fans knew most of the group were movie stars, so they ran after us for miles after we got into the buses, holding up pads and pencils trying to get autographs through the bus windows.

Cairo looked like Disneyland when we arrived. Every building in town was outlined in lights to celebrate the first anniversary of the United Arab Republic. After seeing people along the road dressed as they did centuries ago, leading laden camels and donkeys, the spectacularly-modern Nile Hilton rising up beside the Nile was a startling sight. Welton Becket, the California architect for the hotel, was on hand to take bows. He had set up whole villages to make the furnishings, carpets and draperies, and the job took three years.

There was an inaugural cocktail party for us the first night, and around midnight the Beckets, Miiko Taka, Hugh O'Brian and Bob and I decided to go out to see the Cheops Pyramid by moonlight. High spirited — and high on spirits — we decided to climb the pyramid. Bad idea. Each stone is about five feet high. Not at all suitable for soft Americans — who are high — to climb. Some of the Egyptian boys can get to the top and back in eight minutes. So we tried too. And tried. Miiko and I couldn't even make it up one stone. The taxi driver had more fun watching than any of us had performing.

The next day there was the inevitable desert tent party. It was given in the afternoon this time, and it isn't nearly as exciting by daylight. A dreadful sandstorm helped liven things up. When we arrived by car at the edge of the desert to get on the camels, donkeys or carts for the ride across the desert to the tent, we could hardly see a foot ahead of us.

Evie Johnson, Van's wife, and I jumped into a cart pulled by what turned out to be a rather rambunctious horse. He was more frightened by the storm than we were, and knocked over the man holding his rein and ran away. I managed to jump out, and somehow Evie made it okay to the tent. I got to the tent by foot, running backward. I was trying to get movies of Earl Blackwell and Van Johnson loping along on camels with their overcoats flying in the wind.

The scene at the tent was chaos — Oriental musicians, dancing Arabian horses, magicians, and veiled women telling fortunes in the shifting sands. The tent sides were flapping wildly in the wind and dozens of long-robed men were straining at the poles trying to keep them upright. As soon as a dish was set before us it was so covered with sand we couldn't tell what it was. Didn't taste too bad though. Just a little gritty.

While Van Johnson was doing a belly-dance on the table I heard a hissing sound and turned my head. A grinning devil of a man was standing beside me holding a handful of squirming snakes right next to my face. I'm glad nobody took my picture as I dashed out of the tent and whipped across the desert in the wind.

If the party had been a few days later I probably would have had at least six people following me with cameras. That was when I became a famous movie star. I started out famous, in fact — as Joan Blondell.

It happened because almost everybody on the junket but me was *somebody*. Smiling Egyptians asked us all for autographs wherever we went. When someone tentatively held up a pad and pen to me, hoping they'd recognize the name after I wrote it down, I'd have to say "I'm *nobody*." It was embarrassing to both of us.

But then I was "discovered." I was standing on a windy hill with our host Conrad Hilton, who was wearing a tarbush and Mrs. Earl Warren, dressed in a flowered hat and silk dress. I had on a cowboy suit and Western hat. A photographer rushed up to get a picture of us, with good reason. We looked ridiculous in our varied attire. One of the guides who saw the picture being taken rushed over and held up his pad and pen to me. "May I have your autograph Miss Blondell?" he asked. I gave it to him.

That was just the beginning. Apparently the guide showed my autograph around and soon my fans came running from all directions shoving paper and pencils at me.

The next day at a fashion luncheon the photographers concentrated on my table, not Jane Russell's or Jeanne Crain's. Nor Linda Cristal's or Ann Miller's. Mine. Ada Mildred Anderson Considine's!

eleven

A Belated Wedding Invitation

⋖⟡⋗ They must have mailed my invitation to Joan Blondell by mistake. But never one to carry a grudge, I decided to tag along with Bob to Monaco. He was covering the Grace Rainier wedding, along with the other members of the press, thirteen hundred strong, from all over the world.

For someone who had little chance of getting to the cathedral wedding, I went to an awful lot of trouble picking out an appropriate outfit to take. But one never knows. And it turned out that fortune was on my side. Less than an hour after we got off of the plane, we ran into an old friend, Jack Kelly. He happened to be Grace's father, and a wonderful, wonderful gentleman. So wonderful that he pulled an invitation for me out of his pocket. I was in business.

Actually, for one of the most exciting parts of the Monaco extravaganza one didn't need an invitation at all. *Everybody* was on deck to watch Prince Rainier steam out on his little yacht, "Deo Juvante," to claim his bride from the SS *Constitution.* I watched from Ari Onassis's yacht, "The Christina." It was the greatest vantage post, but I'm afraid I was too busy gawking at "The Christina" to appreciate fully the view of Grace and Rainier. If it isn't the biggest yacht in the world, it'll do elegantly until I see the biggest. Art Buchwald, who was there too, and I explored it in depth. There were fantastically-large suites, priceless paintings, a mosaic swimming pool that could become a dance floor, a yellow seaplane sitting on deck, and a really *King-size* bar.

Ari Onassis told us the bar stools, which looked as if they were covered with drum heads, were actually covered with the foreskin of a whale's penis. (I thought I was back at BION.)

We all had caviar and ouzo, the milky licorice-tasting Greek drink Ari favored, while Prince Rainier sailed out on his little boat to fetch Grace. Then we leaned over the side and looked down — and on the "Christina" we really had to look *way* down — as the "Deo Juvante" proudly steamed back with Grace and His Serene Highness standing handsomely on the bridge waving to their worshipful subjects.

It was bedlam, with cannons booming, planes and helicopters circling and fluttering around, and fireworks exploding overhead, emitting flags. From Onassis's yacht, we bombarded the happy pair with carnations shot out in parachutes. The Prince was beaming and waving, and Grace was holding onto her huge white organdy hat that seemed in danger of blowing away.

While a few lucky newspaper people and a lot of invited guests were attending the official functions during that hectic week before the wedding, the unlucky uninvited ones managed to have a blast anyhow.

The mob's gathering place was the Hotel de Paris, and it was hell getting into even the lobby. The bar was even worse.

Rumors were tossed around like confetti about the many robberies taking place, what the bridesmaids wore to various receptions, and the wedding gifts Rainier was supposed to have demanded from certain subjects and friends. The wildest story was that a lady from Santa Barbara, who had previously been generous in her endowments to Monaco, had offered a silver service as a wedding present and was told that a more fitting gift would be $47,000 worth of radar equipment for Rainier's plane.

To show how fast the rumors traveled, financier jokester George Schlee stood at one end of the long crowded bar and whispered to the stranger drinking next to him that he'd heard it was to be a double wedding, as the Prince de Polignac (Rainier's father) was going to marry Gloria Swanson at the same ceremony. Then George casually strolled down to the other end of the bar. As soon as he took his place, the man next to him whispered: "Did you hear it's going to be a double wedding, and Gloria Swanson and the Prince de Polignac are going to get married at the same time?"

In Monte Carlo that week I became a master at a game many wives must play — "how-to-amuse-yourself-when-your-husband's-working." It was never so painless! At night I'd go with our hosts, the John Pochnas, to the nightclub in the Casino, where we would join Ari Onassis. At the Casino sessions, Lady Norah Docker, the somewhat eccentric wife of a British millionaire, would climb in with the orchestra and play whatever instrument hit her fancy. None hit her talent, but it was fun.

At dawn when the Casino closed, Onassis would walk across the plaza, like a Pied Piper, with the orchestra and those of us who had been sitting with him following along, singing at the top of our lungs. We'd go to an all-night grill for breakfast, dancing on the sidewalk while the orchestra played. It was fiesta time. Anything went!

One night the Pochnas' gave a dinner party for former King Peter of Yugoslavia at Villa Iris, their fabulous villa in Ville-franche-sur-Mer. King Peter hadn't been invited to the wedding or any other official parties. The story went that Prince Rainier, in his moment of glory, wasn't about to be out-ranked by a King, even a former one.

At the villa, I walked out on the terrace with King Peter, and as we surveyed the magnificent house, gardens, swimming pool, tennis courts and guest-houses scattered about, I was surprised to hear him give a low whistle, and softly say: "Wouldn't it be wonderful to afford a place like this — I wonder what it costs!" I later learned that he and his Queen were living in a modest little apartment in Cannes and were completely supported by former subjects and members of the military.

Then came the big day. And after all the extraneous excitement leading up to the wedding, the religious ceremony in Monaco Cathedral was almost anti-climactic. But brilliant, thrilling and beautiful. Grace looked like a story-book Princess, and was radiant in her white gown of lace, satin and taffeta, encrusted with hundreds of pearls and "800,000 transparent sequins." I've often wondered who counted them.

As Grace walked down the aisle to become a Princess, I kept thinking of something one of her mother's oldest friends had told me at a party at the Pochnas'. She said when Grace was a child she used to play-act at being a princess, and even feigned illness now and then so she could be served her meals in bed and act like a grand lady. All her life she wanted to be a princess, and there she was at last walking down the aisle to become one.

Her domain was no bigger than Central Park, but, more important, she was, really was, a Princess.

I noticed that for the Cathedral wedding, Prince Rainier lost most of his "cool." Bob told me that during the civil ceremony in the palace the day before, Rainier just sat there pulling his lip, biting his nails, and not even looking at Grace. At the Cathedral, he looked splendid in his personally-designed uniform, with sky blue trousers and gold sidewalls, and even glanced toward Grace a few times.

After the wedding Bob, with Dorothy Kilgallen, dashed next door to a plumbing shop they'd staked out for writing their stories. I peeked in and saw Bob hard at work sitting on a commode with his typewriter perched on a bidet. I wouldn't dream of disturbing him, so I went on to the palace reception with Gloria Swanson.

Grace, Rainier and the immediate wedding party stood in the enclosure formed by the curving staircase on either side leading up into the palace. Everybody else at the reception milled around the cobbled courtyard, snatching drinks and sandwiches and staring at the wedding party.

The enclosure for the bride and groom was covered with a rug. Grace stood on it next to the Prince drinking champagne, with the train of her gown spread out behind her. Gloria and I stood on one of the stairways watching the proceedings, and noticed that every time the Prince wanted to speak to someone on the other side of Grace he walked right across her train. He didn't do it intentionally — it was just there.

A year or so later when I was spending the weekend with Mrs. Cummings Catherwood in the suburbs of Philadelphia, a lady on the board of a Philadelphia museum came to call. She started enthusing over the fact they had just received Grace's wedding dress to display in the museum. "We just can't understand it, though," she said, "there's something that looks like footprints all over the train. We just can't imagine how they could have gotten there."

The next time I saw Grace, a few years later at a house party in Majorca, I couldn't help wondering whether the footprints had puzzled her. This time she and Rainier seemed completely relaxed — maybe because they were away from the critical eyes of their subjects. Maybe it was just Majorca. We had no critical subjects to escape from, and felt equally carefree.

I remember one party there where the guests took over the orchestra. Elsa Maxwell played the piano, and Rainier and Maria Callas tried various other instruments. Lady Docker would have loved it. I myself should have played solo. My hair that night was an utter mess. I wore my wig over it, but I'm afraid the over-all effect was even less attractive. Actually, I looked just like Harpo Marx. Hedda was quick to agree, and when we sat down at a table on the terrace with Jerry Zerbe, she urged me to "take it off." "For God's sake, no matter how your own hair looks it has to look better than that wig!"

When I hesitated, Jerry yanked my wig off and put it on himself while I ran behind a tree and tried to straighten out my own hair.

Frankly, the wig was more becoming to Jerry than it was to me. He looked kind of cute, and was so proud of himself he went over and danced with Her Serene Highness while wearing it. Several other men at the party then had a go at wearing it. When I got back to New York and gave the wig to a hairdresser to be set, he asked me if it had been in a tornado.

I never did have much luck with false hairpieces. Years ago when I had very short hair I sometimes wore a thick false braid pinned across the top of my head, with my own short hair screwed up in pin curls underneath. I wore it to a cocktail party in Washington once, and Attorney General William Rogers told me how much he admired women with long hair because it made them look so gracious and feminine. So I became gracious and feminine. The sweet, coy southern belle. I did, however, refuse to take my lovely long hair *down* as was suggested. But I always have been obliging, and later, as I was dancing, neither my partner nor I saw a footstool in the middle of the room. We fell over the stool and my braid flew across the room. Right at Mr. Rogers' feet.

No more southern belle for me. I felt more like a wounded bull!

twelve

Bullfight Tickets

✑§§✑ I always sympathize with the bulls.

In spite of the efforts of such aficionados as Rex Smith, Robert Ruark, and even Prince Rainier to make me see the fine points of bullfighting and recognize it as a thrilling sport, I never could. You can't go to any Spanish country without *having* to see bullfights. Otherwise you're left in your hotel room every late afternoon re-reading the only Agatha Christie book you brought along while everybody else goes to the bullfights. That can be deadly.

At a bullfight in Juarez, Mexico, a wounded bull put his head on the fence right in front of me and Mama and bawled so piteously that he had us bawling with him. Almost as awful as that, was the bullfight they staged especially for Prince Rainier and Princess Grace in Majorca.

It's messy enough when the bulls are brave and strong and put up a hard fight before dying. But when they're scrawny and chicken, as they all were that day in Majorca, it's grotesque. One poor bull kept falling down, then struggling to his knees with blood spurting from his mouth and back. I thought the matador was never going to end it. Rainier was trying to explain all the intricacies to me, but I had to leave His Highship in mid-sentence and dash to the nearest ladies' room. On the way back a man told me to wait a minute. Then right in front of me came the horses dragging the carcass of the bloody bull.

The next bull provided some comic relief. The matador's cape got hung on the bull's horns and the bull raced around the arena with the cape spread out over him as if he were wearing it. "That's the only bull I ever saw in drag," was Jerry Zerbe's comment.

The only bullfight of the day Bob and I enjoyed watching at all, was the one conducted by a matador on horseback. It even thrilled me to see him place his own banderillos and effect the kill. There were moments when the angry bull chased the horse and rider around the arena with his horns dangerously close to the horse's rear. The American contingent screamed in unison. Worse than seeing the bulls killed, is seeing those poor scrawny horses ridden by the picadors being hurt over and over. It would have been unbearable if that fine, brave, well-trained dapple gray had been gored too.

Possibly if the picadors were eliminated entirely, bullfights might appeal more to Americans. It would at least make the contest between bull and matador a contest. The job of the picador is to weaken the bull before the matador takes him on. But there's nobody there to weaken the matador! What's fair about that? In fact, if a picador wants to favor a certain matador (and sometimes they do this if the matador has been having a bad time), he can wound the bull with that huge spike to the extent that the bull is practically dead before the matador comes near him.

What upsets weak stomachs the most, though, is the buffeting the picador's horse takes from the bull. That horse is always weak and skinny anyhow like Don Quixote's scabrous mount, and is blindfolded. True, he's more or less covered with padding that hangs down his sides, but the bulls usually manage to get their horns in the horse's exposed belly and it's not unusual to see the horse's entrails hanging out. It would be just as easy to put the padding all the way around the horse so that his belly would be somewhat protected too. Maybe it doesn't happen at all bullfights, but at every one I've ever seen the picador's horse had been knocked down at least once during every fight.

It was the punishment the picador's horse was taking during the last fight of that day in Majorca that drove Bob and me from the arena and back to the hotel. We were sorry we'd left, though, because later on Prince Rainier went down into the ring and made some passes at a bull. He was very good at it, we heard. Grace took movies, but wouldn't let anybody else. If her husband had taken a spill, she certainly didn't want it to be public property.

From what we were told of Rainier's exhibition, he was much braver than movie hero Gary Cooper. I had seen him in a bullring a few years previously at the time of the opening of the Castellana Hilton in Madrid. We went to the finca of Pedro Gandarias near Toledo for luncheon. Afterward, Pedro, who raises bulls for bullfighting, took us all to his miniature bullring, called a plazita, for a tienta, which is a testing of calves for bravery. By testing cows and calves an owner can determine characteristics of a herd. If the cows are rambunctious enough he decides they'll produce brave bulls. The point of the exercise that day was for Pedro's guests to try their hand at the cape-work rather than the kill.

The first two volunteers were Mary Martin and Jinx Falkenberg. Both had on hats and high-heeled shoes, and they looked pretty funny racing around in the dirt arena, mostly trying to avoid the cows. Then Sloan Simpson, who had been living in Spain and practicing at tientas for some time, gave a fine demonstration of all the passes involved.

Dennis McEvoy of Reader's Digest had also lived in Spain for many years, but apparently he hadn't been practicing. He spent at least twenty minutes trying to get the cape disentangled from the cow's horns and hooves and ended up under the cow, still struggling to get the cape loose. When the laughter died down we all urged Gary Cooper to take a whirl at it, and were so insistent he reluctantly went down into the arena. He spent most of his time darting behind the wooden barrera. Pedro came to his rescue, and took one end of the cape. Together they made enough passes at the charging cow to make it look good.

The bullfight festival in Pamplona finally made me lose my Lady Brett complex. The weekend began while I was visiting Robert and Virginia Ruark in their Costa Brava home. We decided to go to Pamplona for the Feria of San Fermín on the spur of the moment, and that's definitely not the way to go to that exciting fiesta. Every hotel room had been booked for a year in advance, so we spent the first few hours there trying to find rooms in a boardinghouse. We were somewhat cheered to learn that even Hemingway sometimes had to stay in a boarding house. We eventually located a room for the Ruarks on one side of town and another for me on the other side. We parted, promising to meet in the plaza, but I never did find them again. They were to go to Madrid the next afternoon and I was to go on to Biarritz for a house party, so it didn't matter too much anyway.

My room was a tiny one on a fourth-floor walk-up and had such a terrible smell that I only took time to drop my suitcase,

~~~~~~

hang up a dress and brush my teeth. Then I went down to the mobbed plaza and luckily ran into Dennis McEnvoy, newscaster Bob Trout and several other friends. We had a drink at Hemingway's favorite hangout, Café Choko, then were caught up in the dancing and riau-riau music that lasted all night. As a matter of fact, it went on for a whole week without stopping. It's impossible to resist, and everybody danced in the streets all through the night.

At seven the next morning came the most exciting part of the fiesta, the running of the bulls. A street leading from the bullpen to the arena was boarded up on the sides, and at 7 A.M. the bulls were released and ran thundering through the street to the arena. Anybody who wanted to, could run along that boarded-up street with the bulls. (The idea is to keep ahead of them if possible. If you don't, it's taps.) The chicken runners got a head start and the brave ones tried to stay just ahead of the bulls. Dennis and I ran with the chickens, but about two blocks of that convinced us we preferred the sidelines. We made a hasty, if undignified, retreat over the fence.

On reaching the arena, the human runners went to one side and the bulls were directed on through the door on the opposite side. Then two or three bulls at a time were let into the arena and the milling kids inside tried their skill as bullfighters, without swords of course. Naturally the runners and would-be bullfighters were mostly young men who dream they are famous bullfighters like Manolete or Dominguin. The stands were filled with spectators cheering the kids on. The kids scrambled around, waving their shirts as capes.

After that everybody went back to the plaza to have breakfast and continue the dancing. The real bullfight wasn't to take place until late afternoon, but I had had it. Suddenly the idea of a nice, clean room in Jock and Brownie McLean's lovely estate in Biarritz was extremely appealing. I hailed a passing taxi and asked what he'd charge to drive me to Biarritz. When we'd settled on a price, I told him I'd give him five dollars extra if he'd go up and pack my bag and bring it down while I waited in the taxi. I'm afraid I only recommend Pamplona at fiesta time for the young and hardy.

One of the few Americans I've seen really enjoy a bullfight was Hedda Hopper, but even in her case I think it was probably the excitement of the crowd in the stands and the ceremony of the opening that appealed to her. There's no question that the entry into the arena of all the participants marching to the stirring pasa doble music is exciting. The lean little matadors strut along with small mincing steps and look so proud in their tight-fitting, colorful costumes!

At a bullfight in Madrid, the first matador dedicated his bull to Hedda by tossing her his hat. Hedda immediately responded by taking off her beautiful big flowery hat and tossing it to the matador. She was a little surprised that he kept it. What she didn't realize, was that of all the items tossed down to favorite matadors by the excited customers, including leather wine-pouches, fans, shoes, hats and even purses, the matadors only keep the women's personal items. They hope the women who threw them will come to their quarters later to claim the items.

Hedda's matador was awarded the bull's ears and offered them to Hedda, but she told him she thought he ought to keep them for his collection. The highest prize a matador can get for his work in the ring consists of the ears, tail and a hoof of the murdered bull. We were glad "her" matador wasn't *that* good.

It seems that Hedda was always generous with her hats. When we left Madrid, we were on the same plane as Louella

Parsons, and Hedda decided the old feud between the two of them was getting ridiculous. She walked the length of the plane and gave her new hat to Louella. Louella accepted it graciously and we all were delighted. Yet the very next night, Louella refused to speak to me because I'd gone to dinner with Hedda. It took quite a bit of juggling to remain friends with both Louella and Hedda. That's one of my proudest accomplishments.

Like Gloria Swanson, Hedda was always the Hollywood "queen." I never saw her outside her own home without one of those beautiful and sometimes crazy hats that were her trademark. She even wore a huge red starched organdy hat and an elegant white dress to a picnic on a beach near Athens once, when Ted Straeter, Earl Blackwell and all the rest of us were in bathing suits. She was probably sorry, though. We were starting to have our picnic and were just wondering what those round white fried things were that the hotel had packed in our lunch basket, when an old fisherman walked up. He sat down right in front of us, and started beating an octopus to death with a rock. The more we begged him to move farther down the beach, the more defiantly he beat the octopus. We wouldn't have minded as much if it hadn't been splattering on Hedda's pretty dress and hat. She was a good sport about it. In fact, Hedda was a good sport about everything.

thirteen

My Badge

꿈 My Olympics Badge — reminds me of every baseball game, football game, wrestling match, boxing match, tennis match, soccer match, etc. match I've ever seen. I think I've witnessed as many athletic contests as the Yankee Stadium has. It's not that I'm a fan. I had to see them if I ever wanted to see Bob. Early in our marriage — for about the first million years — he was a sportswriter, so I became a sports follower.

By 1956 I was just about ready to give up my sports coverage, and let Bob *try* to manage alone. But then he was assigned to cover the Olympic Games in Melbourne, and that was different. For one thing, I had never been to Australia. For another, the Olympics are as much ceremony and spectacle, as athletics. However, it's a lot easier to find an excuse to tag along to Cincinnati than it is to fly across the globe. But I immediately started casting around.

I found the best excuse possible. I had been doing a radio show anyway (some producer friend of ours decided it would be nice money for both of us for me to conduct some fifteen-minute daily interviews with the famous people I've met through Bob's work), so I convinced my sponsor that my background would make me a natural for interviewing the Olympics' participants. He was easy to convince. Even easier was convincing Bob to tell me what questions to ask. When we landed in Melbourne, I think Bob was a little sorry he agreed. But I had the most thrilling experience ever. As we stepped off the plane, a group of newspaper and radio men met us.

"Considine?" one asked.

"Yes," said Bob, stepping forward with a benevolent smile and a willing-to-be-interviewed attitude. I stepped aside for the usual frustrating delay.

"*Mrs.* Considine!" the group said, brushing past Bob.

NBC had forwarded advance notices that they were sending a woman to cover the Olympics. Apparently that's a little unusual. I turned out to be the most willing interviewee those interviewers ever delayed, as I smiled very slightly (I guess smirked) at my husband — patiently waiting on the sidelines.

Once I had satisfied my public, we drove into the city of Melbourne. It was wild with Olympics fever. The Australians are extremely sports-minded anyway. Football games, cricket and horse-races draw 100,000 people all the time. That's fantastic considering the sparse population. Tennis professionals say they do better in Australia than anywhere else. Horse-racing is the biggest draw. There are tracks in every little town, and attending the races becomes an all-day, bring-a-picnic-along occasion for all the country people within miles.

Everybody who could scrounge a ticket piled into the stadium on opening day of the Olympics while hundreds of frustrated would-be spectators milled around outside. My official badge became very precious. As sports-saturated as I had become, I found the opening day enthralling. There was the pageantry of the last runner of the relay team carrying the lighted torch all the way from Mt. Olympus in Greece, entering the stadium and lighting the Olympic flame.

But what about the logistics of the relay race from Greece? That's a rather soaring and inspiring thought — dedicated runners racing through cities and villages carrying the lighted torch, striving to reach Melbourne just as the Olympic Games begin. What happens if a runner gets to a railroad crossing just as the gate is being lowered? Does he stick the torch in the ground and lie down for a few minutes' rest? Who holds the torch while he's going through Customs? And what does he do during those big ocean jumps? Get on a plane in his sweaty shorts and try to keep the torch from setting fire to something? Does he need a ticket? Does he ask his seat-mate to hold the torch while he goes to the john? And what if he arrives in Melbourne an hour before the Games are to open officially? Does he keep running in circles until it's time to enter the Stadium? I'm sorry I didn't interview the runner.

As it was, I interviewed as many athletes as Bob and I could round up, both at the stadium and at the camp in the suburbs where they were housed. By the end of the first week, I'd interviewed more people and seen more sports events than I'd cared to. Then, since, as I said, I had never been to Australia before, I decided on some sight-seeing.

I went to the animal sanctuary forty miles from Melbourne, which for me was more fun than the Games. I alternated between taking movies of the animals and birds and recording — on the tape recorder I brought for the interviews — the various sounds they all made. There were improbable-looking kangaroos, lying on their backs with their feet sticking up in the air or leaping along in great jumps on their huge rear legs. And a whooping crane doing a strange, ritual mating-dance. Since I didn't see any possible mates — and I remembered my pals the belly-dancers — I moved on to the native Australian koala. That was the cutest animal there. It looks like a teddy bear, but isn't even a bear at all. The baby koala hangs onto his mama until he's almost as big as she is, letting her tote him around on her back and find food for him 24 hours a day. And I thought my kids were parasites!

Back home, NBC wouldn't let me use the animal grunts and bird-calls, but they did make terrific background sound for my movies of the sanctuary.

That was the first time I realized the infinite possibilities of a little tape recorder. Bob starred in the best recording I ever made. We've always insisted the other snored, but of course couldn't prove anything.

One night in New York I stayed home and wrote out the questions for the next day's interviews while Bob had a long bull session with his great bull-and-brandy buddy Toots Shor at the restaurant. Bob was asleep and snoring loudly within five minutes of arriving home that night. That's when the great idea hit me. My proof! With malice aforethought and a Charles Addams gleam in my eye, I tippy-toed into the bedroom with my tape recorder and held the microphone right against Bob's nose. Afterward I went into the kitchen and played back the results over and over, rocking with laughter. Then I hid the speaker behind the toaster. Next morning Bob had a special treat with his orange juice. I turned the speaker on full blast.

"What in God's name is that awful racket?" he asked.

"You dear," I replied innocently.

That's when Bob became interested in tape recorders, too. I never knew he was so vengeful. His trick was much meaner than mine. One night when I was sick in bed with a cold, he took his own little recording. I didn't have it for breakfast either. He waited until all the kids and lots of guests were gathered in the bar, and asked them all to listen to one of my more interesting broadcasts. He must have held the microphone even closer than I did.

Far be it for me not to play the revenge game too. Though I state for the record *the following was completely unintentional.* As a matter of fact, I was almost as embarrassed as Bob was. But it was political revenge at its finest. During the Nixon-Kennedy campaign, I was with Nixon all the way. (I never did forgive Eisenhower for answering a reporter's question on Nixon's role in shaping foreign policy, "Give me a week to think it over.") Dick promised that if he won, he'd make one of my favorite fantasies come true — he'd let me sleep in Lincoln's bed. So I did all I could for him — I wore my campaign buttons, went to rallies, stuck a huge Nixon sign in our living room window, etc. Bob, staunchly for Kennedy, reached a few more people through his columns.

Anyway, after the election, I perversely left the Nixon sign hanging. In fact, after a while I forgot about it — you couldn't see it from the inside. The inevitable did happen. One day we heard sirens and went out on the terrace to investigate. Yes, President Kennedy was in town, riding down the street with Mayor Wagner in an open convertible. And yes, Wagner did catch sight of Bob, and the President did look up, and *start* to wave. Slowly his broad smile faded. That's when I finally took my Nixon sign out of the window!

Many pounds ago . . .

And now.

And again now!

The Group—again some pounds ago.

Neither Carrie Munn's husband nor mine thought us very bewitching here.

Meet the real Ivy Baker Priest, former Treasurer of the United States.

Paul Pospesil, Palm Springs, California

I love this one of Louella Parsons and Cobina Wright.

Columnist Mike Connolly brands me at a Las Vegas birthday party.

A funny thing happened to me on the way to Vespers in Cairo.

Al-Gil Akhbar-El-Yom Press, Cairo, Eg

Teaching an obscure young hoofer the twist.

La dolce vita—in Dallas, Texas—with Jerome Zerbe and Earl Blackwell.

Bill Mark, Park Sheraton Hotel, New York City

John Daly explains *his* line to Toots Shor, Bob Hope and me.

The night we lost our fig leaf.

fourteen

A Bon-bon Dish

◆§§◆ The dish is hardly valuable, except to me. It's my first — and only — thank-you gift from a Brink's robber.

Specs O'Keefe first entered our lives through the FBI. They told Bob that Specs wanted to tell all, and further wanted Bob to write the book. So Bob went to Boston to interview Specs. He decided it would be best to have Specs come to New York and tape record the conversations in Bob's office. That seemed the least likely place Specs would be tracked down by the gunmen who were always on his trail.

One night Bob called me from Boston. "The subject of the book is coming down to New York tonight. Call around and get him a room somewhere, then call back and let me know where."

Frank Costello's favorite hotel, seemed like a good choice, but they had no room. I called six other hotels I thought he might like, but had the same problem. It was convention time in New York. I'd hoped to avoid the staid old Plaza, but since I knew Neal Lang, the manager, it became my only choice. When

Neal said he had the room, I suddenly realized I couldn't use Specs' real name. I needed a name fast. I'd been in the midst of a canasta game when Bob called, so I picked one of the foursome, Walter Kiebach. Thinking quickly, I gave Neal the name O'Keefe. I didn't think quickly enough! Walter O'Keefe happens to have been a very popular radio personality. Neal was delighted. And Specs, the next day, was bombarded with calls from Walter's fans. But to show what close tabs the FBI kept on Specs (for his own protection, incidentally), as soon as he checked in, his phone rang. "Hello, Walter, how are you doing?" said the voice of his FBI shadow.

Specs and Bob spent hours together recording the story, and sometimes we all went out to dinner afterward. There's never much sympathy for a man who "sings" but we sympathized with Specs. He had the best of reasons.

Specs was singled out by the others in the conspiracy as the prospective fall guy soon after the fabled robbery. The getaway car, a Ford truck stolen especially for the robbery, was supposed to have been thoroughly disemboweled and its parts scattered. Instead, it was found in still identifiable form on a dump near the O'Keefe home in Staughton, Mass.

On another occasion, Specs was told by one of the top ringleaders that there had been a mistake in the split-up and he had to return $10,000. He refused. He knew there had been no mistake.

However, before he could even spend the booty, one of his less spectacular crimes took him out of circulation. While driving toward St. Louis with a partner, Specs and his pal broke into a store in a small Pennsylvania town to heist some guns. They were caught and arrested. Faced with the prospect of a prison term of several years for that "small-time" caper, Specs turned his $100,000 share of the Brink's bit over to one of his cohorts, one Jazz Maffie.

When he was released from prison, naturally the first person he looked up was Maffie.

Maffie burst into tears at the sight of Specs. The reason wasn't sentimental. He had lost on bad horses — not only his own $100,000 share, but Specs' as well.

Specs seriously considered shooting him. But he remembered that all of the Brink's robbers had shaken hands long before on a pledge to the effect that if any of the conspirators lost his share, through no fault of his own, the others would chip in and make it up to him. Maffie might be needed to bear witness that Specs was eligible.

The mob's answer was to hire Trigger Burke, a cold-blooded New York assassin, to get rid of Specs. Burke nearly succeeded, but Specs had a charmed life. It might be a different story if Specs had remained at liberty. Liberty at that time in his life was not much more than an occasional interruption of prison life. Once again he went back to jail — this time, he was told, because he refused to squeal to the Boston authorities. They were sure he had had something to do with the Brink's robbery.

Specs was questioned repeatedly in prison. His family was under constant surveillance and interrogation. His best friend, a young hoodlum named Johnny Carlson, was apparently murdered for having associated with him. All his pleas to his former buddies for help with legal fees were ignored. They were all prospering, he heard — even Maffie, who had become a successful bookie.

Bit by bit, the FBI agents who visited him at the prison in

Springfield, Massachusetts, wore down his resolution never to blow the whistle. One day he finally said, "All right. What do you want to know?"

The result of O'Keefe's testimony was that all of the Brink's robbers were rounded up, arrested, and given life terms. As his reward for squealing, Specs was released. He remains a very bad insurance risk. The families of the imprisoned men have vowed to get him.

Specs looks like a meek college professor — slim, thin-faced, his "specs" always on. He'd had plenty of time for reading during his long prison stretches, and his coversations are full of literary allusions.

The only times I was ever ill at ease with Specs was during our taxi rides from place to place. I noticed he always sat quite low in the seats. He said it was to avoid random pot shots! I quickly followed suit.

One time Bob and I took Specs to a cocktail party given in Bill Hearst's honor at Luchow's. We introduced him merely as "Mr. O'Keefe." He was utterly charming. Most of the time he sat between Louella Parsons and Mrs. William Randolph Hearst, Sr., carrying on an animated conversation. He even enthralled Serge Semenenko, the Boston banker.

Other times, we'd have dinner at home. Hitchcock had nothing on Specs. In an incredibly mild voice — and with humour — he'd tell the most hair-raising stories.

He said he sensed rather than actually saw Trigger Burke's first attempt to kill him. Specs was driving home one night when he noticed the lights of a following car coming closer and closer to him. We've all had that experience thousands of times, but something prompted Specs to act. As the trailing car swung out to pass him, Specs flung the upper part of his body across the front seat, his left hand still holding the wheel. A split second later, a burst of machine gun fire crashed into the car, streaked right past where Specs head had been, and tore out the windshield.

Specs coolly and gently steered his car over to the left so that it touched the side of the passing car, which was now pouring on the gas for a fast getaway. In that way he was able to stay aligned with the road, without looking up. Then he reached out a foot to the brake, brought his car to a stop and sat up straight again. Alive.

Specs told us that he and the others worked off and on for nearly two years, preparing to rob Brink's. They studied plans and discarded them, before they agreed on the final one. Like a board of directors considering a business report.

They discovered that the electric lines that connected Brink's to a private detective agency, which was always prepared to send armed guards there if the alarm sounded, ran through a sewer in downtown Boston. Someone suggested that incendiary grenades be dropped into the sewer to burn the cables and break the connection. Then Brink's could be robbed without interruption from the detectives.

"Nothing doing," said Specs. "The fire might get out of hand and spread to Faneuil Hall. It's not far from that sewer."

"What the hell is Faneuil Hall!" one of the mob bellowed.

"A very stupid fellow," Specs said of his colleague. "He never even heard of 'the Cradle of Liberty'."

Specs seemed embarrassed to tell us the story. He didn't want us to feel he always mingled with such ignorant people!

They even sent a man to the Patent Office in Washington to study the blueprints on the type of burglar alarm they might encounter at Brink's, and how best to render it mute.

When Bob and Specs finished their work, Bob went to the Plaza to help Specs check out and take him to the airport. It took him ages to come down from his room.

"Sorry," Specs apologized. "I'd automatically packed all the towels, ash trays, light bulbs and the Gideon. Then I remembered you know the manager so I had to unpack them all again."

Specs was a doll of a desperado!

fifteen

A Greek Costume

✍️ While going through a trunk of costumes, I found one I didn't buy for a party. It was either this or a two-hour trip from Delphi, soaking wet or naked.

That trip to Greece began wrong anyway. It was part of an Air France junket to Athens, Rhodes and Paris. And it was supposed to be a sort of second honeymoon for Bob and me. The timing seemed perfect.

This time it wasn't until the day we were set to leave that I got my usual call from Bob:

"Where are you? Why aren't you home packing?" I demanded.

"Sweetheart, it's a long story, but I'll give you the punch line first. I'm in Little Rock covering the school riots."

"But our second honeymoon!"

"Our whole life is a honeymoon, darling, you know that. I have to be here."

"Oh well, I'm going on our honeymoon anyhow, without you! And don't forget your insurance doesn't cover riots!"

"Sweetheart, I promise if I see anybody shooting at me I'll

jump in front of a car. You'll get your double indemnity, darling."

Thus I second-honeymooned alone — with about fifty writers, editors and television people.

The Greek government assigned its top public relations man, a Mr. Cavournidis, to look after our group. He led us through the famous ruins, took us to plays, parties, everywhere. For some reason he seemed particularly fond of me, and suggested I go with him in his car on the sight-seeing tours rather than in the bus with the others. I resisted until Delphi!

There we were led up a steep mountainside to the ruins of Apollo's temple. Mr. Cavournidis told us if we'd all cup our lips and yell in unison, "Apol-l-o-o," we'd get an answer from the god. We yelled. And were answered with the worst cloudburst I've ever seen.

We were on the side of a mountain, drenched, with no place to take shelter. Society columnist Cobina Wright had on a red satin hat, and within minutes she looked as though she had just been in an accident. Great streaks of red were running down her face and dress.

Rosemary Wilson and I saw a little cave. We dashed for it and were washed halfway down the mountain. It was a water drain, not a cave at all.

We all slid and ran down the mountain to the bus. What a pathetic-looking group we were. Our playshoes were so wet we had to wring them out. We all looked like sheepdogs with our hair hanging in straggles around our faces.

We asked the bus driver to stop at the first clothing store he came to. The first one happened to specialize in Greek costumes. The men went behind one curtain, the girls another, and the harassed — but pleasantly surprised — salesgirls kept bringing out every costume in the store until all forty of us on the tour found something to fit. Most of us girls took off our soaked girdles, hose, underwear and dresses, wrung them out, and put them in paper bags along with our shoes, wearing only the costumes. Cobina couldn't quite bring herself to remove "her foundation" and had me stuff dry newspapers inside it all around. Some of us found those Greek shoes with up-turned toes, others went barefoot.

Then I looked at the old bus and at Mr. Cavournidis' car, grabbed Cobina, and rode back in relative comfort. By the time the ridiculous-looking junketeers straggled in from the bus, we were in our regular clothing, sitting in the lobby having tea. Travel-writer Horace Sutton had found my paper bag of clothing on the bus and had tied my shoes, girdle, bra, slip and stockings together, and came in wearing them as a lei. A couple of the boys had bought those ballet-type costumes worn by Greek soldiers and came in doing their version of a ballet dance.

I rediscovered that day how much nicer than buses, cars can be. Cobina did too.

The best event of the whole trip was a performance of Euripides' "Iphigenia at Aulis." We saw it at the ancient outdoor theatre of Herod Atticus at the foot of the Acropolis. In New York it might have seemed melodramatic, but in its native habitat, it was spellbinding.

Whenever the actors moaned or cried, the audience moaned and cried too. The setting itself was very conducive to deep emotion. We sat on the rough-hewn stones that have been used for aeons. There was a luminous full moon, against which loomed the most spectacular edifice in the world, the brilliantly-lighted Parthenon.

That incredible evening was our last in Greece. The next day we were to leave for Paris.

For one young mid-western newspaperman in the group, it was a first trip abroad. His favorite "sight" was a full-blown young belly-dancer he'd found in a small nightclub on the outskirts of Athens. She, in turn, was enchanted with the idea of going to America with a "reech American." He was neither "reech" nor available, but why mention your weak points?

Just as our plane was about to leave, the steward noticed one unaccounted for belly-dancer. He insisted she deplane.

Our lovesick young hero decided if his girl couldn't go, he wouldn't either. There was a moment of indecision while the two of them walked back toward the airport building. Then three of our men took action. They ran out and grabbed the defector and carried him, struggling and yelling, back into the plane.

A couple of years later Bob and I had a more successful try at a Greek second honeymoon. This time it was a junket for the breaking of ground for the new Hilton Hotel in Athens. Cobina was there too. I couldn't resist bragging a bit to Bob about my Greek conquest. At the opening night ball, Bob had the pleasure of meeting him. Mr. Cavournidis rushed up and hugged me and said, "I've been asking everybody here, 'where is my beautiful Cobina Wright,' and here you are at last." Then he turned to Bob and enthused "And this must be *Mr.* Wright — what do *you* do, Mr. Wright?"

"Not a damn thing since I invented the airplane," said Bob, coldly.

sixteen

Mir I Druzhba

~§~ Bob and I went on Sabena Airline's first jet flight to Moscow, and the then new peace and friendship slogan — "Mir I Druzhba" — was in full bloom. All our smiles were returned, and the friendly, helpful people we met made the language barrier less difficult.

Nobody except the Intourist guides and a few headwaiters spoke a word of any language but Russian — not English, French, Spanish or Italian. But, of course, there's no earthly reason why they should. In any case, we really did appreciate our guides. These young men and women are remarkably capable. They helped us with everything — sight-seeing, shopping, getting theatre tickets (and that can be tough). We could have gone any place we wanted to alone, but, frankly, we had no desire to struggle when our guides made life so easy.

Also — perhaps because we were on a junket — we didn't have to use the usual coupon system. We could spend as much as we wanted, and pay with Russian money.

For some reason, most of us were surprised by Moscow's gay

night life. The big hotels — the Mockba, National and Metropole — have huge dining rooms which are jammed every night. The Russian people would laugh and drink and dance to the music of big orchestras, which played mostly American music they'd learned from the short-wave radio.

The "in" place was the Praha, with a restaurant or nightclub on each of its four floors. Caviar and vodka flowed, but the latter, contrary to our pre-set notion, does not flow like water. You can't just say "I'd like a vodka." You have to order a definite number of drams. We chose four because it's always been lucky for us. It turned out to be a nice average-size drink.

Nor can you get anything like a Bloody Mary. At least, we couldn't at the time. They didn't even seem to have tomato juice. One waiter brought me a whole tomato, but the yellowish liquid I squeezed out, plus the seeds and pulp, killed my taste for Bloody Marys in Russia.

Evening or cocktail dresses are out, both for tourists and natives. If you wear one, you'll feel terribly out-of-place. When we were there the style seemed to be long skirts, sweaters, and flat, rounded shoes. Of course, it might have been different at private parties, and, like our styles, it might be different now. Anyway, I hadn't known about this before the trip and only had high-heeled shoes with pointy toes with me. I felt like you'd feel if you wore wooden shoes down Fifth Avenue.

While I danced with several of the Russian men, it turned out I wasn't nearly as popular as Bob. When each man I danced with returned me to the table, he leaned over Bob. I assumed, to thank him for the delightful pleasure of having danced with me. Not at all. They were showing him their money and making signs about either buying his suit or changing their rubles for dollars.

We finally caught on that the Russians jammed the restaurants, nightclubs and theatres because there was nothing else for them to spend their money on at that time. At least, none of the things we save up for — TV's, cars, freezers, etc. So they just spent it having fun. That's not a bad idea at all. They seemed to spend money very freely on the things they could buy. GUM, a mammoth department store that covers several blocks in Moscow, was always mobbed from opening to closing time, with long queues at each counter waiting to buy everything from expensive enamel teacups to Fabergé spoons.

The kids proved an exception to the "no-English" rule. Whenever our car stopped on our sight-seeing tours we were immediately surrounded by children. Their words were "Kent cigarettes," "pens," "postcards." I still don't know why they specified Kents. Neither does the owner of Kents cigarettes, though he was delighted when I told him of the Kent fame. An American newspaperman stationed in Russia told us the kids love to see picture postcards of American cities, and the ball-point pens are not available there. The urchins were always chased away by whatever adult Russian happened to be nearby. They seemed determined not to take anything from us in the way of gifts. Our Intourist guide looked so longingly at my cigarettes, I offered her one whenever I smoked. She'd accept it only if I'd take a piece of chocolate from her. I gained ten pounds on that trip.

We were put up at the Mockba Hotel. If we'd had a choice we would have stayed at the National just across the square, because it's supposed to be the only relatively comfortable hotel there. Our suite of rooms had several interesting features. The windows were nailed down and only a very small aperture at the top could be opened. We couldn't decide whether this was done to keep the Russian winters out or the hotel's inmates in. We didn't mind the early Grand Rapids furniture, but it was nostalgic having a bathroom exactly like the one in Papa's first drugstore.

When it came to room service, the language barrier was formidable. At breakfast time one of us would get dressed, go down to the Intourist office in the lobby, tell someone there what we wanted for breakfast, then go back to the suite and hope it would be delivered. Once when it didn't come, we went down to the dining room only to find we were too late. I was starving. And so the American capitalist — as the waiters must have told their wives — was scrabbling around the tables for food, picking up the bread and fruit former diners had left.

We couldn't help noticing that the women seemed to do all the dirty work. They cleaned the streets — and with such short-handled brooms that they had to bend over double. Some were quite old too. They also drove the streetcars, changed the street lights, ran the elevators — in fact, except for waiters, I never saw any men working at all.

When I mentioned this to our Intourist guide she was quite emphatic. "The women work because they want to," she said, "they are equals with men."

(That kind of "equal," who needs?) "But what do the men do?" I asked.

"They build the buildings, for one thing."

"But we've passed dozens being built and I haven't seen any men."

"They're working inside," she said with finality.

Toward the end of our stay in Moscow, our guide herself brought up the subject again and told me I saw more women working than men just because there are more women than men.

"You know, we lost a lot of our man-power in the war," she said.

She took us to the many former churches that had been converted to museums. Some of the older Russians still took off their caps and crossed themselves before entering. We were told about a Canadian priest named Dionne who surreptitiously conducted Mass in his tiny apartment, so Bob and I found our way over there one Sunday. Chairs were lined up in the living room and about twenty people attended Mass with us, mostly from the Belgian and French Embassies. A little Belgian boy was receiving his First Communion that day. After Mass, we all went into the kitchen and had coffee with the priest. As we left the apartment building we noted we were all clocked off by a policeman at the gate.

The Kremlin Museum, which is actually called the Armory Chamber, is filled with memorabilia of Czarist days — the court dress, the golden coaches, the fabulous Fabergé ornaments, the ermine-trimmed velvet robes, the jeweled crowns and gold dinner services. It's always crowded, and to go through it you have to take off and check your shoes and wear cloth overshoes. That's to protect the marble floors.

I know of no country that offers better entertainment than Russia. It's almost impossible to get tickets for the beautiful Bolshoi Theatre, which alternates between ballet and opera; for the Stanislavsky Ballet; for the wonderful puppet show and the circus — in fact, Intourist is a visitor's only hope for obtaining them. I loved the puppet show and the circus. The latter has only one ring but has more daredevil acts than Madison Square Garden. Popov, Russia's favorite clown, is the funniest ever.

I advise you to wear a sweater under your coat when you go to any kind of entertainment in Russia. They insist you check your coat. Not because of the tips — they don't accept them. Maybe because of concealed weapons. All I know for sure is that the theatres are freezing.

Watching the changing of the guard at Lenin's tomb late at night is eerie. When we went, Red Square was completely deserted except for the two guards standing silent and stiff as ramrods by the tomb. Day and night two such guards stand, facing each other with guns at their shoulders, on either side of the reddish-brown granite mausoleum. They remain absolutely rigid, not even moving their eyes, for an hour's hitch. Then they are relieved by two other guards.

Bob, Ben Grauer and I stood in the silent square by the mausoleum just as the clock struck two. We heard the metallic clang of boots on the pavement that grew louder and louder as the two new guards, accompanied by an escort, neared the tomb. Without a sound except the clanging of boots, the changing of the guards was effected. Then the two men who had been relieved marched off with the escort. The heavy boot-steps became only an echo, and all was silent again. Ben recorded the whole thing and it was one of his most exciting broadcasts from Russia.

Stalin was sharing the tomb with Lenin when we were there. During the few hours each day when they could have company, an endless line stood patiently waiting to shuffle through. We'd been told by Intourist that Americans can go to the head of the line but we thought it would be nicer to wait our turn. In just a few seconds a policeman spotted us and conducted us to the head of the line anyhow.

The Russians were visibly affected as they viewed the bodies, and sobbed audibly as they filed by. We were impressed, too, by their remarkable state of preservation. They both looked as if they could have died that very day, and, amazingly, what looked like blue veins stood up on their hands. I understand the tomb was closed once a month so the inhabitants could be brushed off, shaved and fixed up.

Our last night in Moscow we had a fun-time dining at the National Hotel. The headwaiter knew it was our last night, and apparently told the whole staff. Before we left, we were surrounded by every waiter and captain in the room, and then the headwaiter brought out a tray filled with shots of vodka. Everyone lifted their glasses to us, and said, "Mir I Druzhba." Then they said something we didn't understand. The headwaiter explained they wanted us to know that they liked us and hoped we'd come back.

Before we left for Leningrad we began a task that was to consume much of our time for the rest of the trip. I bet you think it's easy to buy caviar in Moscow. It isn't at all. We needed some desperately. Before going on the trip, we'd asked restaurateur Jan Mitchell what he wanted us to bring him as a wedding present. "Oh, some good Russian caviar would be nice," he said, making it easy for us. He too thought it would be as simple as buying a hotdog in Coney Island. As plentiful as caviar was in restaurants (we even had caviar sandwiches for fifty cents on the train to Leningrad), it was nonexistent in stores. Our guide took us to store after store in Moscow without success. We even had to give up a lot of our sight-seeing time for Project Jan's Caviar. Our guide finally told us we might have better luck when we got to Leningrad.

We had only two days in Leningrad. The attractions there took second place to that damn caviar. In between stores, we went through the Hermitage Museum, a mammoth green and white building with a thousand rooms that was the former winter palace of the Czars. The name Hermitage was adopted during the reign of Catherine the Great who, like Garbo, wanted to be alone. It now houses one of the greatest art collections in the world, one room alone containing 25 Rembrandts. As many as 16,000 visitors a day go through the museum, but not many Americans. A crowd followed us the entire time we were in there. "They want to hear what you talk like," our guide explained.

In Leningrad too, many of the churches are now museums. St. Isaac's Cathedral has been left exactly as it was in the days the city was called St. Petersburg. It's filled with huge malachite columns. While we were there I thought of our friend George Schlee, who used to say, "I was born in St. Petersburg, went to school in Petrograd and got married in Leningrad without ever leaving town."

Lovely old St. Kazan's Cathedral, a miniature St. Peter's, now contains a replica of Sputnik III and a huge bas-relief of the other side of the moon. It has been turned into a chamber of horrors. Our guide didn't care for the pictures of priests and nuns in outrageous postures any more than we did. "Let me take you instead to one of the nice things we have here," he urged.

He took us to a noon matinée of "Sleeping Beauty" given for 400 ballet students at the Kirov State Opera and Ballet Theatre. This was formerly the Marlinsky Theatre which sponsored Chaliapin, Sobinov, Pavlova and Ulanova. Sitting next to us in the box that day were the grandson and great-great-grandson of Rimsky-Korsakov and the sister of Shostakovich.

After the ballet, we resumed our endless search for Jan's caviar, and were rewarded late in the day. We found a small out-of-the-way shop that had beautiful big, loose, gray caviar on display. I bought a two-pound can, which the shop-keeper packed in a back room, and was surprised — shocked! — that it cost $50, even in Russia.

The guide told us to keep the caviar cold, so that became our next big project! It meant getting the hotel to put it on ice, and, trickier yet, having ice packed around it on the plane home.

When I wasn't worrying about the caviar, I kept thinking about our trip and about Russia all the way home. There's something about Russia that's depressing. It's hard to explain, but there's always a point in your relationship with a Russian when all communication ceases. The rest is in pantomime, pointless.

Maybe it's something you said inadvertently that offended, something as innocent as "I certainly miss seeing an American newspaper." To the Russian, that can only mean that you are indirectly repeating the imperialistic lie that there is censorship in the U.S.S.R. Or you may run into some senseless impasse as Bob did on his first trip to Russia. The censor's office called him to task for writing that Khrushchev was "as comfortable as an old shoe." He meant it as a compliment, of course. But the censor wanted to change it to *new* shoe. *Old* shoe, to him, was a reflection on either the Soviet standard of living or Khrushchev's wardrobe.

It's depressing not to be able to take a Russian aside and say, "Listen, Ivan, we want the same things in life that you do: a job, family, friends, a home, enough to eat and drink, comfort and nobody breathing down our necks. We don't like war any more than you do. Why can't we just be friends? Why can't we do things together — like going to the moon as a team or something, instead of us both going broke getting ready to fight each other?"

You'd like to do something like that, but you know if you do, it will somehow sound like propaganda to the Russians and, what's more disturbing, to you.

So you find yourself restricted to the most innocuously general talk. "Yes, the Kremlin *is* beautiful on a moonlit night." "Yes, Van Cliburn certainly is a great hero in the United States." "Yes, the permanent Fair on the outskirts of Moscow is magnificent."

Yes, yes, yes. You find yourself saying it over and over again, because to say no to almost anything — anything from "Have another vodka" to "Don't you agree that our nylons are superior?" — is to break off relations.

You skip over inconveniences which, at home, would prompt you to write a letter to the editor. You do so mainly because the Russian people all around you accept all those difficulties. You hear about the slipshod construction of the endless rows of new apartment houses in the area around Lenin Hills and the University. But you know if you asked a person who lived there how life was in his place, he'd assure you that it was the kind of life the Czar must have lived. But he would never ask you to see for yourself.

You might animatedly exchange stories about children with a young Intourist mother, but try to send the unseen child a box of candy as a present, and the mother may become angry and tell you that she can very well afford to buy all the candy her child deserves.

So, if you ever go to Russia, don't be disappointed if you don't make any lasting friendships.

Also, don't buy any caviar.

Though I did manage to get mine home ice-cold, it wasn't worth it. A few days after I gave Jan his caviar, I ran into him and asked about it. "We gave it to the cat," he said, "it was little and black and not at all good." So, I spent all that precious time shopping for a cat!

seventeen

The Maracas Are Empty of
Jumping Beans

◆§◆ Cuban maracas may not be as tasty as Russian caviar, but they sure were easier to get. You could have gotten as many as you wanted at the airport in Havana. People sent them instead of cards. But then, they're not very useful. I never did find many gift-giving occasions for all fifty pairs I brought home "for the future."

I certainly don't need maracas to remind me of Cuba. It was an old Cuba that I knew — beautiful and gay and very exciting. A Cuba before Castro and Communism and the Bay of Pigs — "bourgeois" as hell and lots of fun. A gloriously degenerate Cuba.

Bob and I used to go to Havana almost every winter. Usually, we'd fly down for a few days from Florida. Once we even went just for the night. We were at a party in Miami with Luis Machado, Cuban Ambassador to the United States, when the idea of a night in Havana hit us. Luis rates A-1 as a guide. In one night we went to more nightclubs than we even knew existed in Havana. It was the beginning of the "cha-cha-cha" era, and we all practiced it so diligently that we literally fell into our rooms at the Nacional at 5 A.M.

That was a wonderful old hotel with its huge rooms and spotless marble floors. The outer walls were pockmarked from gun shots. In 1933 Batista's Sergeants revolted against the army officers and used the Nacional as a stronghold. Somebody was always rebelling in Cuba, mostly students, and I half expected the hotel to be shot at again.

Our first night stop would always be the Tropicana, the greatest nightclub I've ever seen anywhere. It was set outdoors in a garden for dancing, and one could wander over to the gambling rooms, or go over to see the show. That beat Radio City, Bal Tabarin and the Folies Bergères put together. Performers appeared from the top of trees, from runways spaced with great white urns off to the side, from above the stage, from behind, everywhere. I remember one incredibly talented group of musicians — Los Chevales de España. All could sing and all could play every instrument in the orchestra. Luis Tamayo, the featured singer, was the handsomest man I've ever seen.

Then on to the Floridita, where the frozen daiquiri was invented, and you'd meet everybody you knew. And some that you knew only in your imagination. Like Hemingway, who'd be holding court from his special corner. A Cuban combo dressed in white ducks and frilly shirts provided the rumba background.

I'm afraid my reaction to Cuba's famous cockfights is as negative as to bullfights. But at least in Cuba you had a choice. I saw only one — fortunately. Barry was in Cuba with us, and the little barbarian wanted to go. I'm sorry I didn't let him go alone. What's fun about two scrawny roosters with steel spikes on their feet clawing out each other's eyes and ending up as bloody, trembling heaps in the ring!

The worst experience we ever had in Cuba was in Varadaro. After the beach that day we went to an exotic little restaurant we discovered all by ourselves. Delicious, except for the bad case of "tourista" that followed dessert. We wanted out. Havana seemed like a haven. To us — and to all the passengers who gobbled up all the available plane tickets. We turned to a friend, Robert Butler, who was then American Ambassador to Cuba. Bob called him and asked if "by any chance" the Embassy plane could come fetch us. Bob was much sicker than I was, but during their conversation I heard myself becoming the invalid. In fact it sounded as if I were dying.

Next morning I felt rather well. I put on a cheerful chiffon dress and a feather hat that looked somewhat like Mt. Vesuvius erupting. I was set for a nice lunch in Havana.

We were standing by the airport door when the Embassy plane landed. Included, to our horror, were two men with a stretcher.

"Take off your hat! Pretend you're sick!" Bob said. "I guess I made it a little too strong." He was right.

I not only had to be carried on to the plane by stretcher, but had to wear a ghastly oxygen mask during the whole trip to Havana. While I was lying there, moaning every now and then for effect, Bob drank it up with my stretcher bearers. I gave him a murderous look every time I caught his eye, so he managed not to look my way very often.

Back in Havana, I made a fast recovery. It was carnival time! There was dancing in the streets, continuous parades, planes zooming overhead releasing colored paper, and a contagious spirit of abandon. Bob Hope took us to see the floor

show at San Souci that night and was lured up on the stage to do
a dance — the first hoofing he'd done in years.

That was my Cuba. The wild waves crashing over the Mala-
con, the Tropicana, dark little bongo joints where in the wee
hours of the morning the owner, cashier and waiters joined the
patrons in a last and wild cha-cha.

When you love a place as I loved Havana, it's hard to believe
that you can never go back. A couple of years ago when Castro
invited a few American newspapermen to Cuba I asked Bob to
go to the Tropicana again for old times' sake. He was sorry. The
garden was dirty, strewn with paper and trash and there was no
dancing.

What happened? How could a place so completely, and apparently so happily, dependent on us become, for a time at least,
our very worst enemy?

Most Americans rooted for Castro when he was fighting Batista's troops in the hills. We believed what we read about him:
that he was fighting for a more democratic Cuba, one that would
narrow the terrible gulf between the very rich and the very poor.

Bob and I had been exposed to a pretty good example of that
chasm between the classes on one of our trips. A rich Cuban
sugar and rum tycoon invited us to have lunch with him "at the
plantation." The first "entertainment" of the day was to watch
the workers cutting the sugar cane and carting it to the mill. The
people were in rags, horribly overworked, their children ran
about like poor abandoned animals.

Then lunch. It was held in a grotesque rococo castle that had
been in our playboy friend's family for two or three generations
He had imported a New York blonde right out of Central Casting for the occasion. The lunch was something Henry VIII
would have ordered. During all of those courses, our host talked

about how much sugar he owned. Finally, after he had mentioned a figure like "a million tons," or something like that, the babe spoke up:

"That's a lot of sugar . . . dad-dy," she simpered.

The poor people in the fields must have heard his bellow of delight.

Well, he's gone, and a lot like him.

But Castro soon showed the world that he was far from a modern Simon Bolivar. He staged public trials and shootings that stunned his American supporters. He clamped censorship on the press and radio, and expelled or jailed all who raised their voices in protest. He broke contracts with United States firms that had enjoyed long and friendly relations with Cuban companies.

Why?

Bob asked him that question at a press conference. Castro replied that American banks and industries with heavy holdings in Cuba had treated him like a flunky when he came to power. On top of that, he said, the United States Government would not ship free arms to him ("to protect us against the enemies of the revolution") as we once had given such aid to Batista.

"I then tried to purchase surplus weapons from you," he told Bob. "You refused to sell to me. I didn't know what to do. Then I met a diplomat from Czechoslovakia. He offered to send me anything we needed. The Russians have done the same. Why shouldn't I be their friend?"

I can't answer that. But I miss the laughter; laughter that once flourished like sugarcane.

The maracas are empty of jumping beans.

Adios, Havana.

eighteen

Passports... Out-of-date

કર્ષ Foreign sounds, sights and smells overwhelm me as I leaf through these outdated passports with the corners cut off to indicate they've expired. Each immigration stamp in them brings back a random memory . . . the loud church bell shattering the silence of the piazza in Capri . . . the effluvium prevalent in the Casbah of Tangiers . . . the clack of Mah-Jongg that you could hear for miles around rest houses in Kowloon . . . the tinkle of wind-chimes all over the Orient . . . the dank smell of an Egyptian excavation . . . the stench of old urine surrounding the street latrines in Paris . . . the creaking of a thousand windmills in Majorca . . . the sputter and roar of Vespas disturbing our sleep in Rome . . . the eerie sight of the unfinished city of Brasilia . . . the stamping of Gypsy flamenco dancers in Granada . . . the quiet shuffle of hundreds of feet marching during Santa Semana in Seville.

It all began back in 1935 when I got my first passport. I needed it for a trip abroad on the maiden voyage of the ill-fated SS *Normandie.* Something was wrong with the boat from the beginning. She shuddered so violently that everybody's cheeks and fannies shook and bobbled as they walked along the decks.

I was traveling tourist class and shared a stateroom with two college girls I hadn't known before who were violently seasick the whole way. Naturally I avoided the stateroom as much as possible. That was easy because I met up with a swinging little group of young people — as I was *then* — and our sole objective for the trip was to find ways to break into first class. It took a lot of climbing and hiding but we managed it every single night. What fun — what forbidden fun — to watch the floor shows and movies and dance with the first class passengers.

The only other boat trips I took to Europe were the time Bob and I crossed on the SS *Queen Elizabeth* for our wedding anniversary in London, and the maiden voyage of the SS *United States*. We were already *in* the first class sections both those times. It wasn't nearly as much fun.

But we were a gay group on that maiden voyage of the *United States* . . . racing all the way over to break the record held by the *Normandie* . . . emerging as "fastest ship afloat."

Our last night out, almost everybody stayed up all night to be on hand when we passed the point at which we'd know whether we'd broken the record. It was about five in the morning when we got the happy news. Meyer Davis's band went out on deck and all the passengers, in every kind of garb from pajamas to black tie, joined in crying, patting each other on the back, and singing "The Star Spangled Banner." Then, with Meyer leading us, we snake-danced all through the ship, singing and laughing. About fifty of us wound up having breakfast on the floor of my stateroom.

I remember that Ed and Pegeen Fitzgerald brought along their beloved cats. Apparently they take them everywhere. For some reason the ship had no arrangements for cat passengers, nor could the Fitzgeralds keep them in their room. *Felis catus* landed in the elegant dog kennels. A sign, "The Dog House," hung at the entrance, but one morning we were all greeted by a new sign, "The Cat House."

After my last two boat trips I gave up on that means of travel. To me, the four extra days it takes isn't worth it. There's nothing much to do once you can afford first class. Most of our trips to foreign lands are on press junkets anyhow, usually for the inauguration of new flights or the opening of new hotels. "Know Conrad Hilton and you see the world." We've been to Hilton openings from Paris to Puerto Rico.

And we did go abroad quite a bit on our own too, for pleasure with the kids, or for combination pleasure and column material.

To tell the truth, I've traveled around the world enough now to consider heading up a school for neophyte travelers.

The first thing you do before a plane trip abroad, naturally, is to take a weight-lifting course. If you're paying your own way — and the *really* first thing you should do is try to get somebody to pay for you — this will get you in shape to lug your shoe-bag, makeup case, hatbox, the duffle bag of books, magazines, cameras and movie film, and your typewriter, rather than checking it all through with your bags. This can save up to 100 pounds in overweight — if you're not caught carrying it. It's also a good idea to practice in front of a mirror draping the raincoat and cloth coat (which you're carrying along for that express purpose) over the assorted bags you plan to lug on the plane so they won't be noticed.

Unless you're luckier than I am, your husband will refuse to carry one single thing. He'll probably even suggest checking it all through and paying for it, as Bob does.

As your husband checks in at the airport, you stand aside quite a distance with your load while the other bags are being weighed. You can pretend you're looking at magazines and books to buy, though of course you can't buy them because you haven't a free hand to get out the money. As you're checked through the door before boarding the plane, you get in front of your husband and purposefully stride ahead while he distracts the agent's attention with the tickets.

Once that hurdle is over you can relax until just before landing. In fact, if you're with your husband, you can relax from then on. But if you happen to be traveling alone and have struck up a chatty conversation with the gentleman sitting next to you (and somehow they always manage to get you into a conversation even if you pretend you're sleeping or bury your face in a book), there's always that bit about filling out the landing card. His eagle eyes will always watch carefully to see what you write down under "date of birth." I'll never know why even casual acquaintances find a woman's age so fascinating.

I used to wait endlessly until my seat companion had to go to the rest room before filling in that particular item. Now I just boldly write, in front of him, March 2. I don't give the year and nobody has ever questioned it on landing. When your neighbor sees that "March 2" he'll say "AHA, a Piscean, huh?" That will be good for another half-hour's discourse.

Sometimes just to intrigue my seat-mate, under the line marked sex, I've written in "Often" or "Seldom." It seems to idiotic to write "Housewife" under the line asking my occupation, so I've answered that with everything from "Plumber" to "Astronaut."

Usually, when the plane lands, your garrulous seatmate will take pity on you when you go staggering off like a beast of burden and will offer to carry your raincoat. One raincoat and you're stuck with him right behind you when you have to show your passport to the Immigration man. To keep both the person in front of you and your friend behind you from seeing the date of birth in your passport, there's a stratagem. You fumble in your purse for a cigarette until the person in front of you is too far ahead to crane back for a look. Then, to keep the new acquaintance behind from getting too close to see, you assume the stance of someone who has just thrown a bowling ball, leaning forward and stretching your right leg back as far as you can while mumbling something about being cramped from the plane ride.

Retrieving your other bags as they come through on the moving ribbon can be quite simple. Use only very bright-colored baggage, like red or yellow, and have it all alike. Once you've pointed out the first one to the foreign luggage handler, you hold up two, three or four fingers to indicate how many more just like it are coming. Also have in your hand a dollar bill, and the handler will quickly round up your luggage and you'll zip right through Customs. Don't ever make the mistake of buying blue canvas luggage with red leather trim. I had that kind once and so did 90 per cent of the other travelers.

If you want to save time don't take along too many bags, either. Once, on a tour through South America with William Randolph Hearst, Jr. and his wife Bootsie, we wasted hours just counting bags. The Hearsts had 19 with them, including two very long black cases that looked like coffins. They contained Bootsie's long evening dresses. At every stop we'd have to get extra cars just to lug the luggage.

One evening while we were having a cup of coffee in the airport at Rio de Janeiro, waiting for the plane taking us to Montevideo, a Varig public relations man asked us what bags we wanted in the cabin with us. We pointed to the little pile of air-line bags beside us and said "All of them." He misunderstood and thought we meant all of our bags. We had 25 all together. The plane was a half hour late taking off and when we boarded, we saw why. They had taken out some seats in the forward compartment, moved paying customers back, and stacked and tied all 25 bags in there. We had to squeeze — and I mean squeeze — in among them. Varig, by the way, is a great airline to take. Their caviar and champagne are divine.

If you're hopping around Europe by plane and want to keep both seats for yourself so you can relax and stretch out, there's a clever gimmick that's always worked well for me. Say you've managed to get both seats for yourself at the first point by stashing all your portable luggage on the second seat. When the plane stops at the next point to disgorge and assimilate passengers, you again have the problem of someone wanting to sit down beside you. The trick is to unfold the air-sickness bag and hold it noticeably in front of you when the new passengers start getting on. They'll take one look and sit as far away from you as possible. Of course, if the plane has a full load, you're dead.

The ideal way to fly the ocean from New York to Europe or back is to fly in tourist class at night and out of season. The plane will be only half-full and you can take out the arm rests and lie across all three seats in great comfort all the way over.

Going through Customs in Europe has become quite easy. They seem to be mainly concerned about how many cigarettes you've brought. You've already foreseen that exigency by spreading packages of cigarettes all through your suitcases, purses, coat-pockets, etc.

Some Customs officers seem a bit anxious about travelers carrying guns. If one of your pals at home who collects antique guns asks you to bring one or two home from Europe, by all means get small ones that will fit into your suitcase. You can explain those away fairly easily. But try to avoid rifle-type guns that you have to carry over your shoulder because they're too long for your suitcase. Explaining them can be very difficult.

Start out by discouraging gun-collecting in your children. I didn't, and the result was Dennis, the guy with enough old guns to "win the West." Naturally, in Europe he expanded his already beastly collection. Getting through Customs was a cinch with the smallish ones he'd acquired up until we reached Geneva. Just as we were leaving, our host — and friend — Gerald Gross, gave Dennis his now-favorite rifle. It wasn't really very old and was definitely too long to go into any of our bags. Since he didn't give it to Dennis until we were at the airport ready to take off for Paris, there was no way to wrap it. By unanimous family vote, I was elected to carry it!

When we arrived in Paris I marched off the plane first, carrying the gun over my shoulder. That is the handiest way to carry a rifle. I was instantly seized by several policemen and rushed to an office in the airport, with Bob and the boys dashing wonderingly after me and my captors. After much explaining, we were allowed to leave the gun in bond and go on our way.

We got the gun out of bond as we were leaving for London, and since we still had no wrapping, I had to carry it the same way. The same thing happened at the London airport.

Getting arrested can get boring. You might, on second thought, tell your gun-collecting friends — or children — to do their own dirty work.

Actually, the English Customs officials are pretty fussy even about ordinary luggage. They just can't understand why anyone would bring so much perfume in from Paris unless she plans to sell it. I get around that by telling them I bathe in it. They seem to think it's a good idea.

The Customs officers in New York, when you return home, are the only ones likely to give your bags a thorough going-over. If you're wearing a sable stole or mink coat and expensive jewelry, they'll probably assume you've bought couturier clothes in Paris and jewelry in Rome and will completely dissect your bags. If you're innocent and want to save time, it's best to wear your most bedraggled clothes. You should also look sweet, innocent and frank, rather than scared and nervous. The Customs men don't seem to be particularly concerned with souvenirs, scarfs, perfume and gloves. It's the big game they're after — Paris clothes and jewelry. Another diversionary action to keep them from prolonged rummaging through all of your bags is to wear a low-necked dress and keep bending over to pick up some imaginary object.

Of course, an easy approach is to stay more or less within the $100 limit and put all of your purchases in one bag which you hand to the Customs man.

If you don't get to Europe often and want to stock up on enough perfume, gloves and bibelots to last until your next trip, there's a fairly legitimate way to exceed the $100 limit. All the perfume and glove shops in Paris recommend it, for what that's worth. You just have the shop wrap each bottle of perfume or each pair of gloves separately, and have it shipped home in a small package marked "Gift package, value under $10."

The only hitch is that you can't send these packages to yourself — remember they're "gifts." You have to address them to various members of your family and friends, and hope they'll be turned over to you eventually. You'll have to write to the addressees that these "gifts" are not really *theirs* — they're for *you*

when you get home. No doubt you'll feel so cheap you'll decide
to send each of these friends a bottle of perfume for herself too.
So your bill has doubled. Much more than the cost of duty, or
even the same perfume at your home-town store.

There's a solution if you have a dog. Some friends named
Brown have a mongrel named Daisy. "Daisy Brown" has been
receiving the loveliest little gift packages from all over the world
for years. All she wants in return is one quick sniff. If you plan
to try this system, just see that none of your dogs is named
Rover, Fido or Spot.

The very toughest Customs men in the world are those in
Honolulu. It's through them that you have to pass if you're returning from the Orient. And if you're returning from the
Orient, they naturally assume you're smuggling in articles made
in Red China. Every purchase you make in Hong Kong has to
be accompanied by a statement that the article was made in
Hong Kong, not in Red China. Unfortunately, if you've been
lucky enough to find an ancient hand-embroidered wedding
skirt in Thieves' Alley, no such statement is available. It was obviously made in China, but long before it was Red. Sometimes
the fabric you choose at the little tailor's to have your best suit
copied was made in Red China. That's a problem, but one girl
I know found a solution. She wore three made-to-order suits and
a wedding skirt under her own suit when she waddled off the
Pan-Am plane in Honolulu. It's true she nearly died of the heat
while going through Customs, but the understanding Customs
man helped hurry her through. He thought she was pregnant.

Bugs Baer once gave me a wonderful idea by writing in the
front of his passport "President Roosevelt" where it asks whom
to notify in case of death or accident. He was given special attention and rushed through Customs and Immigration all over

Europe. Bob Hope wrote in his passport that Louella Parsons was to be notified. "If she finds out," was his reasoning, "she'll tell everybody else including my wife." Well, I went them a step further and wrote to notify the Pope. Aside from the "red-carpet" potential, a few prayers in my behalf if I did meet with accident or death would be nice. A few close calls, though, made me swing back to Anny Haller, our housekeeper as the one to notify.

The system has possibilities for references too. Remember in the old days how we had to get visas for most of the countries we visited? Well, at the Italian Consulate in New York, on the form we had to fill out, I gave as references, Pope Pius XII and Cardinal Spellman. I turned the form in at the desk and sat in the crowded room to wait my turn. My name was called instantly, and I was ushered with great deference past all the glaring people ahead of me into a room to meet the Consul personally. We chatted a bit about "my friends" the Pope and the Cardinal, and I was given my visa. Also invited back to a cocktail party the next night.

That had worked so well, I tried it again when filling out an application to rent a new apartment. This time instead of giving as references my pals the Al Strelsins, Rosie Netcher and Frank Milan, I added Mayor Wagner to the distinguished company of the Pope and the Cardinal. To my utter shock, a week or so later, we got letters from Cardinal Spellman and Mayor Wagner enclosing copies of glowing testimonials they'd written the real estate people on our behalf. That was when Bob stopped my game.

Enough, though, about circumventing airlines, Customs, etc. Here's a travel hint for your arrival at your destination. Unless you speak French, Spanish and German fairly fluently, don't! That old saw about "the natives appreciate our making the effort" is bunk. They do appreciate it, if we speak their language well. And they appreciate it even more if we don't bore them with a tortured rendition of a language we studied in high school umpteen years ago.

English happens to be a required subject in almost all European schools and has practically replaced French as the international language. You'll find almost all shopkeepers and waiters speak English. Many a time I've struggled along through a whole luncheon order in my execrable French, only to have the captain coldly say "Thank you, Madame. And will you have wine with your luncheon?"

The best idea is to speak English slowly and to enunciate carefully. Most foreigners are more likely to understand that than their own language spoken haltingly and badly. Taxi drivers are the one striking exception. They refuse to understand anything we say, no matter what language we use. I first discovered this in Paris. I was staying at the Ritz Hotel, and when I'd get into a taxi I'd try saying it their way — "Reetz otell." He'd give me a blank look. Well, there's only one other possibility with those two words! "OK, Ritz Hotel." Still blank. Finally, I'd do what I should have done in the first place — print out Ritz Hotel on the back of an envelope and show it to him. "Ah," he'd say, his face brightening, "Reetz otell!" and off we'd go. You can imagine my fate once when I stayed at the Castiglione Hotel! It's best always to pretend you're a deaf-mute with foreign taxi drivers and show them a slip of paper with your destination written on it.

To someone who was not brought up speaking French, that language seems more than mildly eccentric. English is so simple, so straightforward. But French . . . take the number eighty, for instance. Why couldn't they think of a simple word for eighty? Why four twenties . . . quatre vingt? And when they got to ninety, a trauma! Four twenties en . . . quatre vingt dix — three words instead of one. Cooler heads prevailed for the big number, and a hundred is simply cent. If nothing else, you should learn these numbers. You'll want to know what you're being charged for your purchases.

A last hint, for wives only. Be *READY* to go anywhere, any time. Keep two bags stashed in the closet, one packed with summer clothes and another packed with winter clothes. Have your makeup kit filled with an extra supply of cosmetics. Have an extra hair piece all set and ready to pin on. Keep your passport up to date. Then when your husband calls from the office and says, "Sorry, dear, I just found out I have to go to Alaska (or Florida, or Europe or Timbuktu) on a business trip today . . . I'd have liked to take you along, but of course you won't have time to get ready for a week's trip on such short notice," you're prepared.

"Oh, but I *am* ready, darling, and I'd *love* to go along. I'll throw your things in a bag and meet you at the office in an hour."

So what if he's surprised (dismayed?), you will get to go. That's exactly the kind of notice I got before my first trip to Palm Beach.

What a place — the money . . . the beaches . . . the money . . . the parties . . . the money . . . the theatre. . . .

nineteen

The Lotus Eaters

෨෪ඁ Yes, the theatre. I remember opening night of Frank Hale's Royal Poinciana Playhouse eight years ago. A superglamorous event, even for that old dowager of resorts. The Playhouse, which has to be one of the most beautiful and elegant small theatres in the world, and the glamorous Celebrity Room under the same roof, gave the gold-and-Rolls-Royce coast a whole new impetus for social activity during the theatre's ten-week season in late winter.

A different play with changing casts is presented each week, and the winter residents in Palm Beach fight to get permanent seats for the Monday night openings. Not necessarily out of love for the theatre. The real buffs show up at the nightly performances and four matinees the rest of the week.

You see, opening nights are dress-up — way up — occasions that give all the local belles an opportunity not only to show off their own new couturier dresses and their latest diamond necklaces, but also to see what the other girls are wearing.

The Monday night routine is for the theatre-goers to give or attend dinner parties in the adjoining Celebrity Room. It's usual to ignore the frantically flashing lights indicating the curtain is going up until around 9 P.M. Then they stroll through the foyer and exchange greetings with friends and watch the current celebrities being interviewed on TV. They all arrive late, to be seen, and to see the curtain held until they're in their places.

During intermission they all stroll back to the Celebrity Room for a drink or another cup of coffee. Sometimes they don't bother to go back to the theatre after the first intermission. They've already seen and been seen. Or, if they do go back, they get up and leave whenever they feel like it. Sometimes there's only a smattering of audience left when the curtain goes down. Needless to say, actors have come to dread these Monday night openings. Helen Hayes was so incensed over seeing half of the seats empty when her play ended the first night that she threatened not to appear again. Hale must have used magic in persuading her to stay on. Though she was glad she did, when she noted the rapt attention of the non-first night, non-couturier, "out" crowd.

One season when horse-breeder Liz Whitney arrived in Palm Beach with her purple helicopter, two boats and six poodles, she went to the opening of a new musical called *Chrysanthemum*. It's the easiest way to case the action and find out who's in town. A great way to meet old friends. Liz is so gregarious and amusing she's always a most welcome arrival in town.

When the first intermission ended, Liz and her husband Colonel Cloyce Tippett decided to stay on in the Celebrity Room talking with friends until the show ended. They were at the bar when Patrice Munsel swept into the room. Liz rushed over to her: "Patrice, darling, imagine meeting *you* here. What-ever are *you* doing in town?"

It's only fair to say that as star of *Chrysanthemum* Patrice did wear a kooky wig and *was* dressed as a hoyden. . . .

Opening nights, though, are no true indicators of exactly how celebrity-conscious most Palm Beachers are. They lionize the stars of plays, the artists who exhibit at the numerous galleries, and the speakers who appear at the Four Arts forums. When such artists as Simon Elwes, Count Quintanilla and Bernard Buffet visit Palm Beach to exhibit their collections, local hos-tesses make the most of the opportunity to give large soirées in their honor. On opening nights of new exhibitions, Wally Find-lay of the Findlay Galleries and his associate Simone Karoff not only offer champagne and cocktails, but also a buffet of the na-tive food of the artist exhibiting — Spanish fare for Quintanilla's showing, and French for Buffet's, Italian for Piero Aversa, etc.

I think I had the pleasure of meeting the most celebrity-con-scious of all Palm Beachers. Once — and only once — Robert Goulet sang at a charity ball at the Breakers. He had been flown down and paid a huge stipend, and notice of his appearance helped make for a run-away sellout. He did intend to give the audience their money's worth. He sang for half an hour, and walked off to thunderous applause, fully planning to return and sing for another half hour. (This, of course, is routine with night-club singers.) As Goulet left the floor, a socialite jumped up from her ringside table, took a flying leap at him, wrapped her arms around his neck and tightly clamped her legs around his middle. Like a baby chimp clinging to his mother.

Goulet continued on out to a small reception room still car-rying his burden. Since I and my pal, Frances Moody Newman,

had a hand in luring him to Palm Beach to sing at the ball in
the first place, we followed them out.

Goulet was leaning on a table with the socialite still clamped
securely on him and was urging her to disembark. He was getting nowhere.

"If you get off, he'll be able to go back and sing some more,"
I said.

"Yes, please let him go back inside," said Frances.

"You're just jealous," she replied, "I saw him singing
right at you."

Crazy! But we pleaded some more.

"No." She was determined.

In desperation we ran and got two assistant-managers of the
hotel to help pry the lady off. By then the applause was dying
down. It took a full fifteen minutes for the two strong men to
free Goulet and by then the orchestra had given up on his returning and had resumed their dance music.

Goulet beat it out an open door leading to the front grounds
of the hotel.

"Where are you going?" I asked.

"New York, as fast as I can."

I never could convince him that his was a must unusual experience in Palm Beach.

Besides, the local socialites usually favor royal celebrities like
the Duke and Duchess of Windsor and the Kennedys. During
the years when President Kennedy used Colonel Michael Paul's
Palm Beach estate as his "winter White House," the most
avidly-courted hosts and hostesses were the ones who knew the
Kennedys and entertained them — the Charles Wrightsmans,
Colonel Paul, the Earl E. T. Smiths, the Arthur Gardners, Chris
Dunphy and the Laddie Sanfords. Likewise, long before and after

the winter sojourns of the Duke and Duchess of Windsor in Palm Beach, their local friends are plied with invitations to parties so those party-givers will, in turn, be included in events planned for the Windsors.

It's usually unfair to generalize about a city, but Palm Beach does seem to have a pattern of life that's quite circumscribed. It hardly varies from year to year. The residents are a hodge-podge of very old "old guard" society who speak only to each other and go out only for affairs at the Everglades or Bath and Tennis Clubs, or possibly opening nights at the Royal Poinciana Playhouse.

Then there are the "Swingers," both "social" and "semi-social," who think it's a dull day if they go to at least three parties and end up dancing at the Colony, the Celebrity Room or O'Hara's. This group tries to stay on the invitation list of such swinging hostesses as Mary Sanford, Theresa Anderson, "Sugar" Weissman, Betty McMahon, Gregg Moran, Estee Lauder and Ann Mitchell Anderson.

Lastly, there's the sporting crowd who spend their days golfing, fishing, yachting, playing backgammon or gin rummy, or flying over to Grand Bahama for a little gambling.

Palm Beach, seen through the eyes of occasional visitors, is a place where the women say to each other, "Who are you taking to the party tonight?" — not "Who is taking you to the party?"

It's a place where every charity ball brings with it teas, lunch-eons and cocktail parties honoring the ball committee for weeks beforehand, and more money is spent on the parties than is raised at the ball. . . .

A place where the residents are so publicity-conscious that several newspapers and magazines and David Field's "Palm Beach Annual" thrive by just running pictures instead of news

. . . Where a square dance given by Mrs. Merriweather Post at the Everglades Club takes precedence on the front page over a missile shot. . . .

A place where the flower arrangement a visitor sends a hostess seldom contains lilies because those were already bought up for funeral sprays. . . .

The most crucial problem that ever arises in Palm Beach is a scarcity of male escorts. It's a city of wealthy widows and divorcées, but it's hard for a woman to move around socially without any men. The word's gotten out, and an increasingly large number of young men who can get up the price of a sports outfit, a dinner jacket and a plane ticket converge on Palm Beach in season. If they make the right connection they don't have to spend another cent from then on. Looks, intelligence and manliness are not essential. Dancing ability and the gift of flattery help. These young men are invited to be house guests of the lonely ladies usually in the guest-house or pool-house, and their hostesses pick up all the tabs for charity balls, theatre tickets, meals and even new clothes, if necessary.

These men are also provided with cars, which make it possible for them to escape and seek more pleasing — probably younger — companions occasionally. Now and then such a young man can ease in on a permanent basis. Sometimes it works out well for both the lonely ladies and the impecunious young men.

An indication of the wealth concentrated in Palm Beach is the fact that 500 residents own yachts. Probably the best-known one, until Chicago sportsman Leon Mandel gave it to the University of Miami, was the "Carola," named for Mandel's lovely wife. I'm sure it saw more "high" cocktail guests than high seas during "the season."

The newest and biggest yacht anchored in Palm Beach is the

"Southern Breeze," recently bought by A. J. Newman, a wealthy English winter resident. Frank Sinatra and his Mia made the yacht famous during their courting cruise, and the handsome 170-foot ship is now Palm Beach's newest tourist attraction. The Newmans plan to base the yacht in Monte Carlo during their summer vacations.

The man who owns the most yachts in Palm Beach is Jim Kimberly, of Kleenex fame. Kimberly was called "The Gray Fox" by sportswriters when he was in car racing, because of his short-cropped steel white hair, so all eight of his yachts have the name "Fox" in some form. His favorite is a 90-foot job called "The Gray Fox," which is worth half a million dollars and costs $10,000 a month to keep up. God save Kimberly and his yachts from a cure for runny noses!

Before you start thinking "comes the Revolution, Palm Beach will be the first to go," remember all this is only the superficial facade of Palm Beach — the side that is played up in slick magazines and seen by visitors. True, there is phenomenal wealth there, and the residents are spoiled. Sure, social life is important. But if you stay long enough, you can see below the brittle exterior. There are plenty of solid business people in Palm Beach who go to work every day. And in the last couple of years there have been signs that art can compare with openings. The residents themselves have taken to painting, with a sellout exhibition of the work of the Whitney-Vanderbilt clan.

The churches are filled every Sunday. And more charity is dispensed in Palm Beach, probably, than any city of its size in America. A great many of the wealthy women who *could* spend their time only relaxing, do spend it instead helping in hospitals and working for charity. When the theatre season is over, Frank

Hale stages several events in the Playhouse to raise money for various charitable groups.

It isn't all fun and games. Mostly, but not all. And it *is* a spectacularly beautiful place, where the lotus-eating life can be much more inviting than cold reality.

I may even move there when I win the Irish Sweepstakes!

twenty

The Duchess and a Tiny Dog-Carrier

⋙ I can't believe we brought Nicole, the Duchess of Bedford, from London to New York in this tiny dog-carrier!

Our Duchess isn't the kind of royalty that makes Palm Beachers flip. She's a Yorkshire terrier. We bought her while we were visiting the original Nicole and her Husband Ian, the Duke of Bedford, at Woburn Abbey outside London. Nicole the first, said "Why not let me be her godmother, and name her after me?" That's why such an unprepossessing little Yorkie bears such an illustrious name. We call her Nikki for short.

That particular visit was the first time Debbie and Bob spent a weekend at Woburn Abbey. I'd been a frequent visitor and had already clued them on what hip and amusing people the Duke and Duchess are. We arrived at tea-time. That sounds like a drag, but not at Woburn Abbey.

Tea was served in Nicole's bedroom, and on her bed, almost covered by a scramble of newspapers, magazines, dogs and a radio was Bedford's son Robin, the Marquis of Tavistock. Robin was recovering from a hernia he acquired doing the twist. The same thing had happend to his father, the previous year, at one of our twist parties. Apparently it's hereditary.

Nicole's daughter Agnes was lying on the floor playing with Mr. Magoo, their Yorkie. Agnes was wearing a Sherlock Holmes cap and riding breeches, an outfit she wore the entire time we were there. The Duchess, Nicole, was rolling about the floor playing with Robin's baby son Andrew, Lord Howland. Debbie and I sat on the floor for our tea, occasionally slipping cookies to a sleek whippet named Mercurio and a mournful basset hound named Nicky. It was a scene out of *You Can't Take it With You,* especially when Nicole, as soon as she finished her tea, lit up a cigar and tried to get Mercurio to take a puff.

The Duke laughingly pointed out to me the new curtains and draperies in Nicole's bedroom and bathroom. After a previous visit, I'd had the unmitigated gall to write in my "Diplomat" column something to the effect that despite the grandeur of the part of Woburn Abbey open to the public, the private living quarters indicated genteel poverty. I guess I was going on the theory that even a mouse can look at and criticize a king. But instead of being angry — as I would have been — over the ingratitude of a guest, Ian just bought new curtains. What a guy!

Bob and I were given a huge bedroom at the front of the castle overlooking the lake, while Debbie was put in a smaller, but just as charming room farther down the hall. Only it was a little haunted. While we were having breakfast with the Bedfords next morning, Debbie said, "I just can't understand it. You know I took Mercurio to bed with me last night. I locked the door and went to sleep with the dog right beside me on the bed. About three in the morning I was awakened by a scratching *outside* the door, and when I unlocked the door and looked out there was Mercurio trying to get back *in*."

No problem though. We had brought Debbie up to like ghosts.

Ian had to open up part of Woburn Abbey to paying sightseers in order to amortize a five-million pound tax bite on the estate. Quite often he or Nicole conduct these tours personally, and nobody enjoys them more than Ian himself. Apparently he feels that if he has to raise the money for taxes in this fashion, he's going to get a few laughs out of it. The ribald and outlandish remarks he makes about the portraits of his forbears keep the paying customers tittering.

We went along with Ian on one of the tours and thoroughly enjoyed walking within the roped-off lanes admiring the suite once occupied by Queen Victoria and Prince Albert (paintings and sketches by both are on the walls). We saw the rooms occupied by Ian's grandmother, "The Flying Duchess," who was one of the first women to pilot her own plane. One day she flew off, never to be heard from again. Also shown on the tour was a room covered with fabulous Chinese hand-painted wallpaper that was put on in the eighteenth century; a State Dining Room with its priceless Sèvres china and gold tableware; a grotto completely covered with seashells; and a vast array of paintings by Rembrandt, Van Dyke, Hals and others.

Ian has gone out of his way to make his paying customers happy. You can picnic on the beautiful grounds of the estate, where there's a lunchroom, nursery and an amusement area. While we were there, a movie picture company was shooting "The Iron Horse" on the grounds. Every morning, as we looked out of our bedroom window, we feasted our eyes on the grazing herds of cows and deer, on the picnickers peacefully munching on hard-boiled eggs, the costumed extras, shouting directors and puffing trains used for the movie. A wild and crazy mélange. Another time, Ian riled the landed gentry of England by allowing part of the estate to be used as a nudist camp. He has the keenest sense of publicity.

The Duke's proudest possession is the collection of 22 Antonio Canale (commonly called Canaletto) paintings of Venetian scenes that hangs in his private dining room. That's the one exhibit he knows will overwhelm his guests, and he always sits back waiting for their awestruck comments. As we went in to luncheon, I hoped Bob would notice them, especially a magnificent rendition of the area around Piazza San Marco, and perhaps make an appropriate and brilliant comment. "Best painting of Harry's Bar I ever saw," he remarked! Nicole kindly blamed the pictures. She said they weren't properly lighted, and that she had spoken to an Austrian expert on lighting who promised to stop by next time he was in England.

After lunch we all went for a drive except Agnes, who had to wait for a local doctor to come give her a shot against typhoid. She was leaving for Switzerland in a few days and read that a typhoid epidemic was raging there.

While we were out driving, a gentleman with a little black bag arrived at the front door. The butler, who knew Agnes was waiting for him, said "Wait a moment while I announce you." Then he conducted him to an upstairs bedroom, knocked on the door and left.

"Come on in," Agnes called.

There was the Duchess's daughter leaning over the bed with her fanny exposed. All set for her shot.

"Very interesting," said the "doctor," "now where are the Canalettos you want lighted?"

We all spent much of our time enjoying the antics of Nicole's baby Yorky, Mr. Magoo. He was so adorable we decided to buy a little female Yorky to bring home with us. We had ideas in the beginning of uniting our two great fortunes by breeding Nikki and Mr. Magoo, but distance and size prevented the union. We could have somehow surmounted the three thousand miles between us, but never the size problem. After he was full-grown, Mr. Magoo was still a very tiny Yorky. As Nikki aged, she assumed such large proportions she has been mistaken for another breed of dog entirely.

I can't say we weren't forewarned about that possibility. When we went to the kennel to pick out a Yorky, a wriggly little black bundle of fluff separated herself from the other pups and headed straight for Debbie. Debbie picked it up and they showered each other with wet kisses. "This is the one I want," she announced.

"Oh no," said the salesman, "that's the biggest one of the litter — you'll want one of the smaller ones. That one will never be a show-dog like its father Progreso."

"But I'm not going to show it to anybody but Anny and my friends," Debbie said, on the verge of tears. "I don't care if it grows up into a Saint Bernard. I want this one." So that's the one we got.

Nikki may be oversized, but she has manifold charms to make up for that. When she's happy or greets us on our arrival home, she lifts up her upper lip and gives us a big, dazzling smile. She doesn't seem to have much sense of time, though. I get exactly the same wriggly, smiling reception whether I've been away on a two months' tour of Europe or have gone down the hall for five seconds to dump the trash in the incinerator.

Nikki won us all over mainly because she was such a sharp contrast to the last dog we'd had. Mimi, our immaculately pedigreed black French poodle, was given to us by Perle Mesta. She was the stupidest dog I ever saw. When we finally realized that at housebreaking we were zeros, we sent her to dog-training school — $35 a week! More money than I earned slaving eight hours a day as a government clerk! Just to teach a silly dog to do it outdoors. After two weeks they'd bring Mimi home and say she was perfectly trained. Maybe they had a special set of signals for her. We'd take turns walking her by the hour, past every fire hydrant and wastebasket within blocks of our house. She'd enjoy the walk very much, trying to bite every dog and person we passed, but would manage to hold everything until we got back home to those attractive white carpets. Then back to school for another two weeks.

It never did work out. By the time we'd bought two new sets of rugs and had been sued by the television repair man because Mimi bit him, we were a little desperate. She didn't seem to like any of us, but most of all she hated Dennis's best buddy, Frankie Boylan. Frankie would come to our house at least three times a day. Each time Mimi would perk up, leap and grab Frankie by the seat of his pants. Frankie would run straight through the house to the back door with Mimi hanging on in a horizontal position. At the back door Mimi would drop off, Dennis would meet Frankie in the back yard, and they'd go on their way.

That dog was breaking us, and ruining our kids' social lives. We finally put an ad in the *Asbury Park Press:* "Will give pedigreed French poodle, a wonderful watchdog, to first caller." Mimi probably *was* the best watchdog that ever lived. She never ever stopped barking, and she bit the hell out of anybody who tried to come into the house, even the owners. Such a nice couple showed up for Mimi. I hope they're doing okay. . . .

twenty-one

J. Paul Getty and an Unidentified American Woman

❧ Obviously I kept this Italian newspaper clipping because of the picture, not the caption. It's a couble-spread of me doing the twist at the London Hilton opening with J. Paul Getty. Translated, the caption says "J. Paul Getty, the richest man in the world, doing the twist with unidentified American woman." X!?X!! Oh well, I looked too fat anyhow. No woman looks her best doing the twist.

Getty turned out to be a good twister. I helped teach it to him that night. I remember the first time we met him. We were taken to his great home, Sutton Place in Guildford, England, for luncheon. An awesome experience. But that good old mid-western theory of humanity carried me through. You know how it goes. We're all human — we all have to blow our noses, go to the bathroom, eat and sleep, laugh and cry. Bob Hope helped me out on that occasion, though he doesn't know it. I told Getty a joke — a new one, too — that Bob had just told me. It must have been a great joke, for Getty and I have been corresponding ever since relaying the latest gags. Recently Getty sent me a really gorgeous picture of himself wearing a Beatle wig.

Naturally, before our visit, we had heard all the stories about how tightfisted Getty is. Not true. We were served a magnificent luncheon, with a footman behind each of our chairs. After lunch, Getty took us on a tour of the estate. I kept looking for the pay-phone booth we'd heard all his guests had to use; there's no such animal. In fact, I made two calls to London in his study.

Much of our tour consisted of a search for the keys to the different rooms. All are kept locked. Always. Getty is almost like a little boy about his possessions. When he took us into the great hall that houses his biggest and best paintings (after we finally found the key to it, hid in the chest drawer in the hall), he insisted we stand at a certain point by the windows so we'd get the best view of the room. He was as thrilled as we were over the enormous Gainsborough that covers one wall, and he spent a lot of time arguing why another large painting whose authenticity has been questioned had to be the real original. He made us all walk back and forth in front of Rembrandt's "The Assassin" to prove that the eyes followed us no matter where we went. Bob had to go and crawl under the painting! "You got gypped, Paul," Bob said. "He can't look down!"

On the tour, Getty told us all about the lore of the house and the people who had lived in it, and showed us the big old ledgers containing the place's history. We saw every inch of the house from the bathrooms to the newly-decorated servants' and guest rooms. Getty's personal bathroom is the end. It's all marble and gold. Even the bidet fixtures were gold.

All the master bedrooms looked out over a majestic and infinite esplanade of manicured lawn with wonderful old gnarled trees and a profusion of yellow jonquils. Getty showed us a painting of the house made over a hundred years ago, and pointed out several of the trees still there on the lawn. There's nothing blasé about Getty. He's the billionaire of the world, yet completely entranced by what he owns.

The kitchens, pantries and workrooms seemed endless. I've never seen so many glasses, dishes and pans. Just outside the kitchen door were the kennels where Getty kept the watchdogs we'd heard baying at us as we arrived. They made our Mimi seem like a kitten. Probably the biggest, meanest-looking dogs in the world. They set up another cacophony as we approached them, chained in their wire enclosures. They calmed down when they saw Getty. He let one of them out, and while we all cringed in terror, Gerry petted him, and the dog in turn licked Getty's hand and reared up with his paws on Getty's shoulders. He explained that he has to keep the dogs for protection, and that the fences are all electrically wired for the same reason.

Beyond the kennels were an outdoor pool on the left, and a newly-built marble indoor pool on the right. We spent quite a while in the indoor pool while Getty pointed out to us all the "faces" he'd discovered among the swirls of the marble. He was pleased when we found a few more he hadn't noticed.

When Getty told me he'd had five wives and five sons, I asked him if he planned to marry again. "Never!" he exclaimed. "Tried it and didn't like it." Nevertheless, his household included two very lovely ladies. One was a comely Russian countess, who lived in the house with her young son. She seemed to be in charge of running the house, and on a very high level, indeed. She's the one who usually came up with the missing keys.

The other lady, a beautiful young lawyer, was apparently in charge of running Getty's business and social life. He took her along on all of his social outings, and it was through her that everyone got to Getty — or didn't. She was present the night that picture was taken at the Hilton inauguration ball, and spent most of the evening singing her praises to me. "Can you imagine anyone that pretty also being an absolutely brilliant lawyer?" was the thread of his long discourse. He was right too. She's completely captivating.

During our first luncheon at Sutton Place, I mentioned that the dining room reminded me of the great dining hall at San Simeon, the California home of William Randolph Hearst, Sr. Getty seemed terribly interested, but our conversation was interrupted. When we got back to our hotel in London that night, the phone was ringing. It was Getty. "Tell me," he started right off, "would you say my dining room was larger or smaller than Mr. Hearst's?"

"It's hard to say," I lied, knowing Hearst's was bigger. "The weekend Bob and I spent there only five of us sat at the big, long table, so we felt dwarfed by the room. There were so many people at your table today that I couldn't really tell how big the room was."

"Now how about my library where you saw the Gainsborough today," continued Getty. "Did Hearst have any room that big?"

"No," I answered truthfully. "I've never seen a room that big."

"What did you do in the evening when you were visiting Hearst?"

"Well, after dinner I slipped Marion a drink in the powder room, then Mr. Hearst and I played gin rummy, then I slipped Marion a drink, then I played Monopoly with Marion. Mr. Hearst obviously didn't like Marion to drink. I lost all the games, by the way."

"How come?" he asked.

"Well, Marion whispered to me that Mr. Hearst liked to win at gin rummy, and Mr. Hearst whispered to me that Marion liked to get all the hotels at Monopoly, and I whispered to me that I liked to get invited to the Hearsts."

"And the Hearsts' dining room is probably bigger than mine!" Getty laughed. "But tell me what the grounds are like?"

"Oh goodness, there were thousands of acres surrounding the house, which was on a hill-top, and they were full of wild animals . . . giraffes, buffalo, bears, everything. That's why it was all enclosed and we had to go through several gates before reaching the house."

Then I told him about a funny experience Lloyd Pantages had during a weekend party at San Simeon. One day while Mr. Hearst and Marion were out riding, Lloyd and two other house-guests decided to practice hitting golf balls. Lloyd had one long, hard drive that hit a gnu in the forehead and knocked him dead. The group slunk back to the house and kept very still about the incident. Mr. Hearst is very fond of his animals. They kept even quieter during dinner when Mr. Hearst told them the game-keeper had found one of the gnus dead from a very strange wound — an indentation in the forehead whose cause he couldn't possibly imagine.

It became apparent to me that Mr. Getty greatly admired Mr. Hearst. But when the subject was finally exhausted, he said, "I remember you said you're going to my hotel, the Pierre Marquess in Acapulco. Write and tell me what it looks like, will you?"

"Sure, but why don't you go see it for yourself?" I asked.

"Oh, I haven't even seen my Pierre Hotel in New York. I don't care much for travel."

That's an understatement. I learned later from his close friends that Getty is so terrified of planes and most other modes of travel that he hadn't set foot out of England for years, except for occasional trips to Paris. Even then he didn't trust the planes or the channel boats, and took the *Queen Elizabeth* or the *United States* from Southampton to Le Havre, then went on to Paris by boat-train.

I wonder how he got to Rome, where he recently acquired a 52-room castle, with cannons instead of dogs for protection.

Getty is so mild-looking and soft-spoken that it's hard to imagine his having the drive to acquire a billion dollars. *A billion dollars!* That doesn't seem extraordinary to Getty though. Once when he was being interviewed on a radio show the interrogator asked him if it were true he was worth a billion dollars. "We-ll, I don't know," mused Getty, "I may be worth a billion or I may be worth two billion. But remember, young man, a billion dollars isn't what it used to be."

twenty-two

Plane Tickets to Tel Aviv

꿐꿐 Tel Aviv, a city of violent contrasts . . . a tall, pristine hotel on the edge of the Mediterranean next to miserable immigrant shanties . . . a thriving kibbutz beside an ancient Arab graveyard . . . modern roads and office buildings and rising forests and orange groves . . . nightclub singers and Hebrew sages . . . a proud man with a purplish concentration camp tatoo on his arm beside his strong, carefree son.

A proud city . . . like a mother with a new baby . . . or even like a woman bringing up her children in a sprawling old house in Allenhurst, New Jersey. Yes, a mid-western Protestant, Catholic-convert can identify with the Israeli people. It's easy, for theirs is a universal story.

I had wanted to go to Israel with Bob, who had been there several times, but never did until the opening of the Sheraton Tel Aviv. It's an amazing city. The most interesting part, to me, is the old section, the original city of Jaffa, which has narrow streets, clamorous bazaars and strange, Oriental smells and sounds.

The nightclub singers there chant wailing old Hebrew folk songs accompanied by stringed instruments. The effect is stirring.

The port city of Haifa, which is much older than Tel Aviv, is a beautiful, clean city built on three levels of a mountain, reminiscent of San Francisco. The lowest level, called "the town" or "the German colony," boasts the best restaurant in town. The second level, where the middle class lives, is called "the beauty of the Carmel." That's where the excellent Zion Hotel is. The top level is called "the top of the Carmel," and from here one has an unsurpassed view of the city, harbor, the Carmel range and the surrounding countryside. A stream-lined new funicular, a source of much pride in the city, runs from the top to the bottom levels. We were told that the mayor of Haifa drives all over the city every morning to make sure the streets have been washed down.

The country's only golf course is a few miles out of Tel Aviv in an area called Caesaria. The clubhouse is ultra-modern, but it's set in the midst of Roman ruins built by Herod twenty-five years before Christ. An amusing rule of the club specifies that if a golfer displaces any grass while swinging his club, and happens to uncover any old coins or other relics, he is entitled to keep them as long as he replaces the divot. A lot of archeological buffs in Israel helped themselves to the ruins before Caesaria became a national monument, and you'll find some back yards containing as many columns and historical artifacts as can still be found in Caesaria.

The caves in Nazareth where Mary received the Annunciation and where the Holy Family lived are still there. Our guide was an Arab, and to our surprise, he told us that 150,000 Arabs live in Israel, and the countryside and villages are dotted with their homes. Literally dotted, for all of the Arabs paint their doors or windows blue to keep out evil spirits.

The well where Mary used to draw water is still used by the women of Nazareth, who line up with earthen jugs on their heads just as they did two thousand years ago. Except when the nattily-dressed visitors come to have their pictures taken in front of the well. Then all of the native women scurry away and hide their faces. There's still the old horror of graven images, and a visitor soon learns not even to try to get pictures of these colorful Israelites.

On all sides we saw orange groves where there were only swamps a few years ago, forests in what was barren, sandy ground, housing and factories, all effected by the back-breaking efforts of determined, idealistic people who managed to return to their Promised Land.

Most of the forests were donated by Americans. In some places, a whole forest had been given by one benefactor. In other areas, the forest sprang up tree by tree. For five dollars, a visitor can plant a sapling tree in memory of a friend, and everyone does at least this much to help the country. We planted our tree near Jerusalem, and choose a pine tree in memory of our beloved friend Arch McDonald, the Washington radio broadcaster, whose theme song was "Cut Down the Old Pine Tree." We tried to find our tree during our second visit, but it was hopeless.

Jerusalem is a frustrating city, especially for Christian visitors. Many of the Christian historical landmarks and the Wailing Wall are in the verboten Arab territory beyond the Mandelbaum Gate — a gate that placed in history the name of a tailor whose shop was next to it. There was, however, the climb up Mt. Zion to the scene of the Last Supper.

The streets of Jerusalem are filled with Yemenites in biblical
dress, brushing past the Orthodox men and boys with their long
side-curls.

Tea in the home of David Ben-Gurion and his Brooklyn-born
wife Paula was on the agenda during our trip. It was then that
some of our group were personally indoctrinated to Paula-isms.
Paula is, without doubt, the most talked-about person in Israel.
Surely she's the most unorthodox, forthright and sometimes
undiplomatic wife a head of state ever had. Everyone has an
anecdote about her, but everyone smiles in telling it. They sum it
all up affectionately by saying "She's Paula."

During the tea party while everybody was marveling at the
agelessness of Robert Frost, who was among the Sheraton guests,
designer Mollie Parnis said, "I think we're only as old as we feel,
and I don't feel any older than I did twenty years ago."

Paula said in her cheerfully shattering way, "If you'll take all
the gook off your face, I'll tell you how old you are."

We were told the most widely-quoted Paula-ism the minute
we arrived in Israel. Supposedly, she once went out in her house-
dress and asked the policeman in the pillbox to run to the
grocery store for a bottle of milk.

"But I must remain here and guard the Prime Minister,"
said the policeman.

"Never mind," replied Paula, "I'll stand in the pillbox and
guard — you go to the grocery store."

Another time, she gave the policeman a pat of butter and
asked him to run down to the laboratory to have it analyzed for
quality. It must have been for her husband, for Paula is also
well-known for wifely devotion.

Whenever Ben-Gurion has to take a plane trip alone, which is
often, she packs a lunch for him. The plane food won't do at

all. If she happens to go along, she sends ahead fresh lemons, lettuce and other ingredients, and then goes into the plane's pantry and mixes the salad herself. He likes her cooking so she still does it all. She rises two hours ahead of Ben-Gurion in the morning so she can make breakfast and have all of his clothes laid out when he gets up.

Once when Ben-Gurion was hospitalized for wounds received during the bombing of Parliament, Paula came down with a bad cold and was sent to the same hospital. To keep him from knowing she was sick, she got up twice a day, dressed completely, put on her coat and hat, took her shopping bag, and went to the floor below to visit her husband. Then she went back up, disrobed, and got back in bed.

The final feature of the Sheraton opening schedule was a picnic luncheon at a kibbutz near Nazareth called Kafar Hahoresh. The residents of the kibbutz decorated the dining room with gay streamers and pictures, but the hotel provided the food and drinks. Bob and I, along with the hotel manager, went out ahead of the others in a station wagon carrying the supplies.

We helped unpack and arrange the food and liquor, then wandered around looking the kibbutz over until the others arrived. I noticed several women in aprons and babushkas working in the garden. There was a hoe leaning against the front porch, so when I saw the bus bearing the rest of our party off in the distance, I borrowed a babushka, grabbed the hoe and started working industriously at a flower bed in the front yard, carefully keeping my back to the road.

As the bus ground to a halt I turned around and every person in the bus was leaning out the windows with cameras trained on me. What a priceless movie of a kibbutz woman hard at work they got!

It wasn't until 1965 that I got back to Israel. This time on a junket for the opening of the Tel Aviv Hilton. Since we, George Jessel, the Earl Wilsons and Maxine Mesinger had all been to Israel before, we spent most of our time just having fun rather than sight-seeing with the others. With Jessel around, it's fun all the way.

Although he's raised more money (tens of millions) for Israeli bonds than any other single person, very few Israeli people seem to recognize him. But on that trip they certainly did look at him. Jessel had just returned from entertaining the troops in Viet Nam, and apparently grew very fond of the uniform he wore there. He left it on throughout the Israeli junket — an American army hat, a British bush jacket, khaki Bermuda shorts and knee-length wool socks! Where medals and ribbons would ordinarily be attached, Jessel had his ASCAP pin, his Fraternal Order of Eagles pin and his UJA pin.

If lack of recognition from the people he's done so much for was galling to Jessel, the failure of the upper Hilton echelon to call on him for a speech was even more so. When Connie Hilton invited Jessel to the opening, he said, "I can't go on this one so I'm sending my son Nicky. Will you kind of help take my place?" Jessel, of course, thought that he was to take Hilton's place in the speech-making department. He had worked out one of his best for the big opening-day luncheon. To his horror, he wasn't even seated on the dais, much less called on. Nicky made the speech, and a very good one too.

"Well," said Jessel, "I guess they're saving me for the luncheon at the museum in Jerusalem." At the museum luncheon Jessel wasn't even seated at the head table, much less called on. Nicky made the speech. Even Nicky's wife, Trish, made one.

By now, everyone was as angry as George that he'd been overlooked and someone spoke to Nicky. There was a hurried conference, and it was decided that George would be master-of-ceremonies at the opening of the hotel nightclub. George found a way to strike back. He used his very bluest material. He weakened toward the end, though, and started talking about how much Israel means to him. As usual, the tears flowed down his cheeks.

"How do you always manage to cry on cue?" I asked Jessel later.

"I think about how deaf Sophie Tucker is getting," he said.

Then he told the story about how he was once introducing Sophie to an audience while she waited in the wings. "I want you to meet Sophie Tucker, the last of the red-hot mamas. Sophie's had a sad life though. She was deserted by Sammy Davis, Jr. and left with two illegitimate children, Bobby Baker and Christine Jorgensen."

As he went over to lead Sophie onto the stage, he asked, "Did you hear what I said about you Sophie?"

"Yes," she said. "It was beautiful. I cried like a baby."

One day, we were all taken by bus to the great new Israel Museum in Jerusalem. We saw the Dead Sea Scrolls and the archeological treasures, as well as the highly-publicized garden containing the statuary donated by Billy Rose.

As Bob, Jessel and I wandered through the garden we realized that none of us really appreciated modern sculpture. We recognized nothing at all. A piece of misshapen rock painted red and white was called, to our astonishment, "Mother and Child."

"What did Billy Rose have against Israel," George muttered as we looked for some familiar object. Finally, off to one side of the garden, we saw a huge mobile that looked almost like a working pump. "Ah, I take it all back," George said, "Billy *did* have *some* taste — that's a beautiful piece of statuary." When we got up close, we noted that it not only looked "almost like a working pump," but was one.

"I think I know the exact moment Billy turned against human nature," Bob said. "Remember that time we went to visit him at Mt. Kisco with Mike? Remember the tennis balls?"

All too well. We were spending the weekend with Maggie and Carl Ruff, and we all went over with Mike and Maggie's son Chuck to have lunch with Billy and his wife Eleanor Holm. Billy greeted the kids enthusiastically and made noises about how much he liked children and missed the patter of little feet around the house.

We all had a swim in the pool, then went up to the tennis courts to watch Eleanor, Bob, and Oscar and Dorothy Hammerstein have a game of doubles. The boys stayed at the pool to play.

When the game was over we started to the house for lunch. Billy glanced toward the pool and said, "My God, it looks like the pool is full of tennis balls." It was — hundreds of them. The boys had not only discovered Billy's cache of new tennis balls — they'd also discovered that tennis balls float in swimming pools. Exceedingly well, too!

Ah, "the patter of little feet . . ." That was our last invite from Billy.

En route back from the museum we passed through the town where Samson and Delilah did their cutting up, and stopped, of course, at "Samson's" for a drink.

As we entered, Jessel demanded, "Where's that lady barber?" The customers were more startled by his "uniform" than by his question.

George took one sip of his drink, then lifted it high and sang very loudly "Sweet Ad-o-line." By now the customers were beginning to edge away from us.

"If anybody asks for my autograph I'm going to sign 'Al Jolson' — these squares don't even know he's dead."

What's worse, they didn't even know Jessel was alive!

"Nasser would get a better reception in this country than I'm getting," George grumbled as he marched out.

twenty-three

A Kinescope of Person-to-Person

&§&~ Bob often squawked about the number of guests I
invited to our Allenhurst house, but he was as hospitable as I
was the night we invited about twenty million people to drop
by for fifteen minutes.

It happened ten years ago. Innocently. We ran into Ed Murrow
at Toots Shor's and he said, "You know you're going to have
to give in and go on Person-to-Person eventually. How about
the fall when we go back on the air?"

"Sure, sure, we'd love it," we said and promptly forgot about
it. The fall seemed so far off. Ed didn't forget, though. While
vacationing in Honolulu with the kids we got a nice short
telegram . . . "How about September 21?"

A definite date scared me a little. The kids, too, were torn
between nervousness and pride, but basically they're hams like
their mother.

About a week before "the day," two nice young men named
Dave Moore and Chuck Hill of Murrow's staff came out to the
house to "case the joint." They looked it over and decided to

start the show on the big old-fashioned front porch of the house, then move on to the living room, dining room and bar, and end up again in the living room.

Next, Mr. Moore called me to have lunch with him to talk about clothes and other details. I'd already gone through my wardrobe and decided to wear a slimming, low-necked black sheath and my new black cashmere sweater with a white mink collar. I thought the outfit would look slightly elegant, but country-ish too. That was the first to go.

"Here are the only things you can't wear on a TV show," said Mr. Moore, "black or white or a sheath dress." It seems black and white don't photograph well. Also, you have to wear a full skirt to hide the batteries strapped around your hips, and a high neck to cover the microphone pinned to your bra. The dress must be on the grayish or dark side, but not black.

Meantime the kids began to panic about their lines. Dennis worked himself up into such a state he threatened to run away from home! Barry, on the other hand, was dying for a chance to get home. He was going to Valley Forge Military Academy and wouldn't have made it until Christmas otherwise. A nice telegram from Murrow to General Milton Baker got Barry a 24-hour leave. The school got a plug, and Barry got to parade his new uniform and his new straight back before his neighborhood pals.

I began to panic too when men from the telephone company came a few days before the show to erect a five-story steel tower in the back yard — a king-size jungle-gym. We were going to be beamed to Asbury Park . . . to the Empire State Building . . . to twenty million eager, critical eyes! We couldn't decide whether to tell all of our friends to watch, or to go on a midnight television set-breaking raid.

For several days before "the day" people stopped Bob and me on the street to say, "Well, I'll be watching you Friday," and gave us a reassuring good-luck pat. That helped loads! One pal said, "I hear you're going to lose your fig leaf Friday," which is exactly how it does feel. The enormity of exposing ourselves, our family! At that point, even I would have gladly backed out.

I wanted to look as glamorous as possible, so I went to the beauty shop and told Melanie to make me a few shades lighter than usual so I'd sparkle on camera. The kids got haircuts, and Anny, Rosie and Addie got new uniforms.

Since the house was going to be seen by twenty million people, we decided to clean — really clean. We went through drawers and closets I'd been meaning to get to for a year. Silver got polished, windows washed, porches hosed down. When the crew arrived, one member said, "I hope you didn't go to any special trouble cleaning because we'll mess it all up and dust doesn't show anyhow."

There they came — thirty crewmen dragging in miles of cables and truckloads of cameras. The garage became the control room — and the home of dozens of neighborhood kids who refused to budge all day. Luncheon was served in the garage.

About 2 P.M., Mr. Moore and Mr. Hill, the director, arrived and I suddenly realized something should be done about planning dinner for the crew. Addie and Rosie insisted we should have a real banquet at dinner time. I agreed, hoping that well-fed crewmen would take more pains to make us look good on TV and get our best angles.

One crew member told me that Hildegarde, after *her* Person-to-Person show, served the crew a seated dinner! We added two more courses to the menu.

Just as we started rehearsal, a dozen long-stemmed roses arrived

from Ed Murrow with a "Good luck" card enclosed. That reminded Mr. Moore that we should have flowers on the tables
to hide some of the microphones. So we called Mr. Jameson.
Along with our order, he presented me with dozens of mon-
strously large dahlias — prize-winners all — that he wanted to be
seen on television.

That was just one of many plugs we got in. Everybody we knew
started calling and asking us to sneak in some product or other.
We never counted up, but during that brief show, I recall we
succeeded in mentioning Bob's radio sponsor, Mutual of Omaha
and its president, V. J. Skutt, the milk container a friend was
pushing, an advertising column I was writing at the time for
New Yorker and *Newsweek,* Valley Forge Military Academy,
artist friends John Morris and Huldah, Toots Shor, the kids'
piano teacher Clara Chichester, Ben Wright, and my best friend
Frances Moody Newman.

Along about 5 P.M. I decided to have another try at my wardrobe. I picked out four possibilities, pressed them, and put them
on, one by one, for Mr. Hill's approval. He selected the oldest,
least glamorous one.

Around 7 P.M. a nice young man I hadn't noticed before
said we'd better strap on the batteries and microphones and
arrange the wiring under my dress so it wouldn't show. Bob put
his batteries in his back pocket with the wire going down inside
his pants leg and trailing along the floor behind him. The kids
didn't need batteries or mikes as they were to be shown only
once, sitting at tables in the bar.

The nice young man peered up under my dress and decided my
girdle was the most secure place to pin my batteries. As he was
pinning them on, he said, inclining his head toward the bath-

room, "Remember, every sound you make from now on will be heard by the engineers at CBS."

That did it. I was nervous enough before, but now I had to call him to take off the batteries and put them back on at least six times before the show started. At one point, as I was trying to feign the nonchalance I certainly did not feel while the fellow was on his knees pinning my batteries back on, Barry started into the room.

"Oh, I beg your pardon," he said.

There went my last grain of confidence.

Sometime during the evening we all ate — I think. At 8:30 we had another run through with Moore. At 9:45 we had a short conversation with Mr. Murrow, whom we could never see at any time although he could see us. We were told to look at the camera with the red light on and pretend *that* was Mr. Murrow! At 10:30 we all took our places and waited for the Bette Davis half of the show to go off. At 10:45 we were *on.*

The show started with Bob walking the length of our front porch, and with the camera following him it looked a block long on screen. After saying a few words inside the front door, Bob strolled into the dining room where I was striking what I hoped was a fetching pose in front of our Delft ware and some of the silver we'd received for our recent 25th wedding anniversary.

In a quavering voice several octaves above my normal pitch, and smiling idiotically throughout, I explained about the Delft and silver. Mercifully, Bob said, "Shall we join the children in the playroom?"

Playroom! Anybody with only one eye could plainly see it was a barroom that was normally the scene of drinking orgies.

The ashen-faced children were sitting at two tables in the "playroom," and the ordeal of each saying a few words to Ed Murrow behind his smoke-screen had the same effect on them it had on me — their voices soared upward. Mike talked about his experiences in the Marines, Debbie talked about school, Barry demonstrated how they had to sit at table at Valley Forge, and Dennis talked about his guns. Thank heavens they remembered what they were to say and said it.

Bob and I then strolled into the living room and sat down on the couch for the rest of the interview, during which I got through at least three cigarettes. When Murrow sent us the kinescope I noticed that particular segment looked as though it had taken place during a volcanic eruption or an atom bomb explosion. Too bad none of our friends was plugging cigarettes!

When Murrow finally said those beautiful words "Good-night Bob, good-night Millie," the playroom quickly reverted to its normal state and got a work-out through most of the night. All the neighbors who had been circling the block in their cars or just standing in the yard joined us in celebrating. And what a celebration!

Was it worth it? Definitely. For the kinescope, for the celebration, for that year's supply of precious milk cartons. . . .

twenty-four

Here We Go Again

❧ How completely different a "Person-to-Person" show of us would be today! In the first place, it would have to be in our city apartment rather than in our wonderful old Allenhurst house.

Oh, we were anxious enough to get rid of it once the kids were grown, but it's still a very special house. A house full of children, family dinners, happiness and love.

When the last moving van had left and we got into the car to drive to New York, I glanced back. The house already looked lonely and accusing.

Will the pear tree in the front yard bloom again? Will the portico be covered with honeysuckle and the side yard be filled with lilacs? What will happen to the hollyhocks I planted by the garage?

Will somebody else find "our" tiny patches of violets and lilies of the valley? Or realize that the garden chives make great Sunday morning omelets?

Will there be other gay parties around the big barbecue in the

back yard with a rented juke box blaring? Will some little
boy spend hours shooting baskets in the hoop attached to the
garage door? Will the cedar trees ever again be covered with
Christmas lights?

I hope so.

It would be hard to round up the family for a TV show now.
Mike is running his own restaurant in Sausalito, California.
And Dennis is studying to be a psychologist at the University of
California. Debbie, too, is in college, the only one of our kids
who wants to be a writer. Barry's a television cameraman on the
Merv Griffin show. He married Sue, a lovely Allenhurst girl, as
soon as he began earning enough money. A year later on St.
Patrick's day they gave us our beautiful grandchild, Kelly Ann
Considine.

There's nothing wrong with New York City. We're enjoying
it. They say it'll be even more entrancing when they finish the
place.

The chives for Sunday morning breakfasts are easier to find
than in Allenhurst. You can call the grocer across the street
and a boy brings them around in a package untouched by
human hands. And it's easier still to walk down the street and
have brunch at the Plaza.

We have a balcony big enough to support a wire-legged
table and chairs like the sets Papa had in our drugstores, and
flower boxes filled with little artificial trees that don't need a
$75-a-month gardener. Our pots of petunias self-lift their
beautiful pink faces week in and week out, finding something
invigorating in the soot and noise and disorder of the city.

On a clear night we can see the muggings in Central Park from
our balcony, which holds about six people except, of course,

during cocktail parties. Then it holds up to 100. (Whenever
I serve Bob his breakfast out there, I think of the wife in the
New Yorker cartoon: "Come out and have your soup before it
gets *dirty.*")

Those who agree that New York is a great place to live, but
would sure hate to visit there, will recognize our way of life. One
of the hardest things to adjust to when we moved from a low
apartment on Park Avenue to a higher one on the park was the
lowering of the noise level. There's a special kind of quiet that
can get on one's nerves.

It's a relief now for us to get out into the bustle and din
of the city. We can walk to almost any place we need for
nurturing body and soul. The century-old Church of St. Paul
the Apostle? — two blocks to the left. 21 Club . . . Toots
Shor's? — turn right down to the Americana, then turn left. Saks
Fifth Avenue . . . Best and Company? — a few steps beyond
"21." Shakespeare? — in the park just outside, after dinner under
the stars at Tavern on the Green. Hot pastrami sandwich with
champagne? — the joker from the Stage Delicatessen is there in
five minutes. Drug store . . . Doctor . . . Dentist . . . Garage . . .
Psychiatrist? — right in our building. Broadway theatres? —
walk down Seventh. Carnegie Hall? — around the corner. Bank
. . . Pawnshop . . . Rembrandt for sale . . . Shoemaker . . .
Bookstore . . . Saloon? — around the corner. Bus . . . Cab?
at the door (except, of course, when needed). Club? — across
the street. Ice skating? — in the park. Hospital? — across from
the church. Old Folks Home? — turn left. We plan to walk,
not run.

We don't lose shingles anymore when the great tail winds
of hurricanes from Ada to Zelma sweep up the Atlantic. We

never have any trouble with the neighbors; we haven't any. You don't have neighbors if you live in a New York apartment. Just acquaintances, at best.

On the night of the Great Blackout, while we were working at our typewriters by candlelight, there was a spooky knock at our door. We went out with a candle and there stood a pretty, terrified young woman, tears streaming down her face. She made a nightmarish scene in the otherwise Stygian blackness of the hallway.

"I live here," she said, pointing to the door next to ours. "I was taking a nap, waiting for my husband to come home. I woke up and thought I had gone blind . . ."

She came in and we celebrated her restored 20-20 vision with a few drinks. We found her charming, and her magazine work gave us much in common to talk about as the candles and the Scotch bottle burned lower.

We had lived together, separated by a paper-thin wall for nearly two years, and though we always knew when she took a bath, we had never met or even seen her until now. When she returned to her apartment with one of our candles, to await the long-delayed arrival of her husband, we said what comes naturally to city people: "Let's get together real soon."

We haven't seen her since.

We can't see the sun come up or sink. The tall buildings that line Fifth Avenue and Central Park West hide such miracles. But we see the sun's fire reflected in penthouse windows and know it made it, up and down, and God is in His heaven. At night we look far up the darkened park to the neon glow of Harlem, and overhead there regularly passes Echo I, Echo II and Pegasus — aloof of all in space.

The red, white and blue New York Airways helicopter to and

from Kennedy Airport reminds us as it passes that it's been days, weeks, sometimes months since we shook loose the dust and galloped off to some place across the land or sea. And when we're away, we'll never have to worry about the furnace running out of oil, the pipes freezing, somebody breaking in and stealing my jools (what a cruel trick that would be on the burglar), peeling paint, and the leak in the bar that cleverly eluded every repairman in Jersey.

Still, our grandbaby Kelly makes us wish we had the big old house back. We could take her to the beach in her funny little bathing suits. Or make costumes for her to wear in the beach-club shows as I did for Debbie. We could watch her pick flowers and have fun with her at our huge holiday family dinners.

But what the heck — we can start a whole new era with Kelly the city slicker. There's the Planetarium, the museums and all the shows around town put on for children. We'll teach her to ice-skate in the park, and take her on the Carousel by the Zoo. . . .

Someday she may even ride a camel in Tangiers, and go to a tent party on the Sahara. . . .